# 1 - Year Daily Devotional for Students

# Quiet Time
## One year daily devotional for students

Word of Life Local Church Ministries
A division of Word of Life Fellowship, Inc.
Joe Jordan – Executive Director
Jack Wyrtzen & Harry Bollback - Founders
Mike Calhoun – VP of Local Church Ministries

**USA**
P.O. Box 600
Schroon Lake, NY 12870
talk@wol.org
1-888-932-5827

**Canada**
RR#8/Owen Sound
ON, Canada N4K 5W4
LCM@wol.ca
1-800-461-3503 or
(519) 376-3516

Web Address: www.wol.org

**Publisher's Acknowledgements**
**Writers and Contributors:**

| | |
|---|---|
| Bobby Barton | 1 & 2 Kings |
| Matt Boutilier | Hebrews |
| Cory Fehr | Esther, Song of Solomon, Titus, Philemon, 2 Timothy, Nahum, Malachi |
| Andy Grenier | Psalms, Proverbs |
| Paul O'Bradovic | Revelation |
| Joe and Gloria Phillips | John, Ephesians, Lamentations |
| Matt Walls | 1 Corinthians |

**Editor:** Dale Flynn
**Curriculum Manager:** Don Reichard
**Cover and page design:** Adam Rushlow



ISBN - 978-1-931235-51-8
Printed in the United States of America

# Helpful Hints For a Daily Quiet Time

The purpose of this Quiet Time is to meet the needs of spiritual growth in the life of the Christian in such a way that they learn the art of conducting their own personal investigation into the Bible. Consider the following helpful hints:

**1** Give priority in choosing your quiet time. This will vary with each individual in accordance with his own circumstances. The time you choose must:

- have top priority over everything else
- be the quietest time possible.
- be a convenient time of the day or night.
- be consistently observed each day.

**2** Give attention to the procedure suggested for you to follow. Include the following items.

- Read God's Word.
- Mark your Bible as you read. Here are some suggestions that might be helpful:
  - a. After you read the passage put an exclamation mark next to the verses you completely understand.
  - b. Put a question mark next to verses you do not understand.
  - c. Put an arrow pointing upward next to encouraging verses.
  - d. Put an arrow pointing downward next to verses which weigh us down in our spiritual race.
  - e. Put a star next to verses containing important truths or major points.
- Meditate on what you have read (In one sentence, write the main thought). Here are some suggestions as guidelines for meditating on God's Word:

a. Look at the selected passage from God's point of view.

b. Though we encourage quiet time in the morning, some people arrange to have their quiet time at the end of their day. God emphasizes that we need to go to sleep meditating on His Word. "My soul shall be satisfied and my mouth shall praise thee with joyful lips: when I remember thee upon my bed, and meditating on thee in the night watches" (Psalm 63:5,6).

c. Deuteronomy 6:7 lists routine things you do each day during which you should concentrate on the portion of Scripture for that day:

— when you sit in your house (meals and relaxation)
— when you walk in the way (to and from school or work)
— when you lie down (before going to sleep at night)
— when you rise up (getting ready for the day)

- Apply some truth to your life. (Use first person pronouns I, me, my, mine). If you have difficulty in finding an application for your life, think of yourself as a Bible SPECTator and ask yourself the following questions.

**S** – is there any sin for me to forsake?

**P** – is there any promise for me to claim?

**E** – is there any example for me to follow?

**C** – is there any command for me to obey?

**T** – is there anything to be thankful for today?

- Pray for specific things (Use the prayer sheets found in the Personal Prayer Diary section).

**3** Be sure to fill out your quiet time sheets. This will really help you remember the things the Lord brings to your mind.

**4** Purpose to share with someone else each day something you gained from your quiet time. This can be a real blessing for them as well as for you.

# My Personal PRAYER Journal

"watch, and pray..."

# Sunday

"watch, and pray..."

"watch, and pray..."

"watch, and pray..."

## Family

## Christian Friends

## Unsaved Friends

"watch, and pray...

"watch, and pray...

"watch, and pray..."

## Missionaries

# Monday

"watch, and pray..."

"watch, and pray..."

"watch, and pray..."

## Family

## Christian Friends

## Unsaved Friends

"watch, and pray..."

"watch, and pray

"watch, and pray..."

## Missionaries

# Tuesday

"watch, and pray..."

"watch, and pray..."

"watch, and pray..."

## Family

## Christian Friends

## Unsaved Friends

"watch, and pray...

"watch, and pray...

"watch, and pray..."

## Missionaries

# Wednesday

"watch, and pray..."

"watch, and pray..."

"watch, and pray..."

## Family

## Christian Friends

## Unsaved Friends

"watch, and pray..."

"watch, and pray

"watch, and pray..."

## Missionaries

# Thursday

"watch, and pray..."

"watch, and pray..."

"watch, and pray..."

## Family

## Christian Friends

Unsaved Friends

"watch, and pray..."

"watch, and pray..."

"watch, and pray..."

Missionaries

# Friday

"watch, and pray..."

"watch, and pray..."

"watch, and pray..."

## Family

## Christian Friends

## Unsaved Friends

"watch, and pray..."

"watch, and pray..."

"watch, and pray..."

## Missionaries

"watch, and pray..." "watch, and pray..." "watch, and pray..."

# Saturday

## Family

## Christian Friends

My Personal PRAYER journal

## Unsaved Friends

"watch, and pray..."

"watch, and pray

"watch, and pray..."

## Missionaries

My Personal
PRAYER
journal

# PRAISE LIST

| dATE | aNSWER |
| --- | --- |
| | |

"watch, and pray..."

My Personal PRAYER journal

# PRAISE LIST

| dATE | aNSWER |
| --- | --- |
| | |

"watch, and pray..."

# PRAISE LIST

| dATE | aNSWER |
|---|---|

"watch, and pray..."

# Something for everyone

Some people just can't get enough! That is why we have several dimensions in the Word of Life Quiet Time. Along with the daily reading, content and application questions for each day, two reading programs are given to help you understand the Bible better. Choose one or both.

## Reading Through the New Testament Four Times In One Year

Turn the page and discover a schedule that takes you through the New Testament four times in one year. This is a great method to help you see the correlation of the Gospels and other New Testament books.

## Reading Through the Whole Bible In One Year

Turn another page and find a program of several pages that will guide you through a chronological reading of the entire Bible. Follow this schedule and you will move from Genesis through Revelation in one year.

## The Choice is Up to You

Whether you have a short quiet time, a quiet time with more scripture reading or one with a mini-Bible study each day, we trust your time with God will draw you closer to Him in every area of your life.

# Read through the new testament

## Weeks 1-13

- ☐ Matthew 1-3
- ☐ Matthew 4-6
- ☐ Matthew 7-9
- ☐ Matt. 10-12
- ☐ Matt. 13-15
- ☐ Matt. 16-18
- ☐ Matt. 19-21
- ☐ Matt. 22-24
- ☐ Matt. 25-26
- ☐ Matt. 27-28
- ☐ Mark 1-3
- ☐ Mark 4-5
- ☐ Mark 6-8
- ☐ Mark 9-11
- ☐ Mark 12-14
- ☐ Mark 15-16
- ☐ Luke 1-2
- ☐ Luke 3-5
- ☐ Luke 6-7
- ☐ Luke 8-9
- ☐ Luke 10-11
- ☐ Luke 12-14
- ☐ Luke 15-17
- ☐ Luke 18-20
- ☐ Luke 21-22
- ☐ Luke 23-24
- ☐ John 1-3
- ☐ John 4-5
- ☐ John 6-7
- ☐ John 8-10
- ☐ John 11-12
- ☐ John 13-15
- ☐ John 16-18
- ☐ John 19-21
- ☐ Acts 1-3
- ☐ Acts 4-6
- ☐ Acts 7-8
- ☐ Acts 9-11
- ☐ Acts 12-15
- ☐ Acts 16-18
- ☐ Acts 19-21
- ☐ Acts 22-24
- ☐ Acts 25-26
- ☐ Acts 27-28
- ☐ Romans 1-3
- ☐ Romans 4-6
- ☐ Romans 7-9
- ☐ Romans 10-12
- ☐ Romans 13-16
- ☐ 1 Cor. 1-4
- ☐ 1 Cor. 5-9
- ☐ 1 Cor. 10-12
- ☐ 1 Cor. 13-16
- ☐ 2 Cor. 1-4
- ☐ 2 Cor. 5-8
- ☐ 2 Cor. 9-13
- ☐ Galatians 1-3
- ☐ Galatians 4-6
- ☐ Ephesians 1-3
- ☐ Ephesians 4-6
- ☐ Philippians 1-4
- ☐ Colossians 1-4
- ☐ 1 Thes. 1-3
- ☐ 1 Thes. 4-5
- ☐ 2 Thes. 1-3
- ☐ 1 Timothy 1-3
- ☐ 1 Timothy 4-6
- ☐ 2 Timothy 1-4
- ☐ Titus 1-3
- ☐ Philemon
- ☐ Hebrews 1
- ☐ Hebrews 2-4
- ☐ Hebrews 5-7
- ☐ Hebrews 8-10
- ☐ Hebrews 11-13
- ☐ James 1-3
- ☐ James 4-5
- ☐ 1 Peter 1-3
- ☐ 1 Peter 4-5
- ☐ 2 Peter 1-3
- ☐ 1 John 1-3
- ☐ 1 John 4-5
- ☐ 2 Jn, 3 Jn, Jude
- ☐ Revelation 1-3
- ☐ Revelation 4-6
- ☐ Revelation 7-9
- ☐ Rev. 10-12
- ☐ Rev. 13-15
- ☐ Rev. 16-18
- ☐ Rev. 19-22

## Weeks 14-26

- ☐ Matthew 1-3
- ☐ Matthew 4-6
- ☐ Matthew 7-9
- ☐ Matt. 10-12
- ☐ Matt. 13-15
- ☐ Matt. 16-18
- ☐ Matt. 19-21
- ☐ Matt. 22-24
- ☐ Matt. 25-26
- ☐ Matt. 27-28
- ☐ Mark 1-3
- ☐ Mark 4-5
- ☐ Mark 6-8
- ☐ Mark 9-11
- ☐ Mark 12-14
- ☐ Mark 15-16
- ☐ Luke 1-2
- ☐ Luke 3-5
- ☐ Luke 6-7
- ☐ Luke 8-9
- ☐ Luke 10-11
- ☐ Luke 12-14
- ☐ Luke 15-17
- ☐ Luke 18-20
- ☐ Luke 21-22
- ☐ Luke 23-24
- ☐ John 1-3
- ☐ John 4-5
- ☐ John 6-7
- ☐ John 8-10
- ☐ John 11-12
- ☐ John 13-15
- ☐ John 16-18
- ☐ John 19-21
- ☐ Acts 1-3
- ☐ Acts 4-6
- ☐ Acts 7-8
- ☐ Acts 9-11
- ☐ Acts 12-15
- ☐ Acts 16-18
- ☐ Acts 19-21
- ☐ Acts 22-24
- ☐ Acts 25-26
- ☐ Acts 27-28
- ☐ Romans 1-3
- ☐ Romans 4-6
- ☐ Romans 7-9
- ☐ Romans 10-12
- ☐ Romans 13-16
- ☐ 1 Cor. 1-4
- ☐ 1 Cor. 5-9
- ☐ 1 Cor. 10-12
- ☐ 1 Cor. 13-16
- ☐ 2 Cor. 1-4
- ☐ 2 Cor. 5-8
- ☐ 2 Cor. 9-13
- ☐ Galatians 1-3
- ☐ Galatians 4-6
- ☐ Ephesians 1-3
- ☐ Ephesians 4-6
- ☐ Philippians 1-4
- ☐ Colossians 1-4
- ☐ 1 Thes. 1-3
- ☐ 1 Thes. 4-5
- ☐ 2 Thes. 1-3
- ☐ 1 Timothy 1-3
- ☐ 1 Timothy 4-6
- ☐ 2 Timothy 1-4
- ☐ Titus 1-3
- ☐ Philemon
- ☐ Hebrews 1
- ☐ Hebrews 2-4
- ☐ Hebrews 5-7
- ☐ Hebrews 8-10
- ☐ Hebrews 11-13
- ☐ James 1-3
- ☐ James 4-5
- ☐ 1 Peter 1-3
- ☐ 1 Peter 4-5
- ☐ 2 Peter 1-3
- ☐ 1 John 1-3
- ☐ 1 John 4-5
- ☐ 2 Jn, 3 Jn, Jude
- ☐ Revelation 1-3
- ☐ Revelation 4-6
- ☐ Revelation 7-9
- ☐ Rev. 10-12
- ☐ Rev. 13-15
- ☐ Rev. 16-18
- ☐ Rev. 19-22

**four times in one year**

# Read through the new testament

## Weeks 27-39

☐ Matthew 1-3
☐ Matthew 4-6
☐ Matthew 7-9
☐ Matt. 10-12
☐ Matt. 13-15
☐ Matt. 16-18
☐ Matt. 19-21
☐ Matt. 22-24
☐ Matt. 25-26
☐ Matt. 27-28
☐ Mark 1-3
☐ Mark 4-5
☐ Mark 6-8
☐ Mark 9-11
☐ Mark 12-14
☐ Mark 15-16
☐ Luke 1-2
☐ Luke 3-5
☐ Luke 6-7
☐ Luke 8-9
☐ Luke 10-11
☐ Luke 12-14
☐ Luke 15-17
☐ Luke 18-20
☐ Luke 21-22
☐ Luke 23-24
☐ John 1-3
☐ John 4-5
☐ John 6-7
☐ John 8-10
☐ John 11-12
☐ John 13-15
☐ John 16-18
☐ John 19-21
☐ Acts 1-3
☐ Acts 4-6
☐ Acts 7-8
☐ Acts 9-11
☐ Acts 12-15
☐ Acts 16-18
☐ Acts 19-21
☐ Acts 22-24
☐ Acts 25-26
☐ Acts 27-28
☐ Romans 1-3

☐ Romans 4-6
☐ Romans 7-9
☐ Romans 10-12
☐ Romans 13-16
☐ 1 Cor. 1-4
☐ 1 Cor. 5-9
☐ 1 Cor. 10-12
☐ 1 Cor. 13-16
☐ 2 Cor. 1-4
☐ 2 Cor. 5-8
☐ 2 Cor. 9-13
☐ Galatians 1-3
☐ Galatians 4-6
☐ Ephesians 1-3
☐ Ephesians 4-6
☐ Phil. 1-4
☐ Colossians 1-4
☐ 1 Thes. 1-3
☐ 1 Thes. 4-5
☐ 2 Thes. 1-3
☐ 1 Timothy 1-3
☐ 1 Timothy 4-6
☐ 2 Timothy 1-4
☐ Titus 1-3
☐ Philemon
☐ Hebrews 1
☐ Hebrews 2-4
☐ Hebrews 5-7
☐ Hebrews 8-10
☐ Hebrews 11-13
☐ James 1-3
☐ James 4-5
☐ 1 Peter 1-3
☐ 1 Peter 4-5
☐ 2 Peter 1-3
☐ 1 John 1-3
☐ 1 John 4-5
☐ 2 Jn, 3 Jn, Jude
☐ Revelation 1-3
☐ Revelation 4-6
☐ Revelation 7-9
☐ Rev. 10-12
☐ Rev. 13-15
☐ Rev. 16-18
☐ Rev. 19-22

## Weeks 40-52

☐ Matthew 1-3
☐ Matthew 4-6
☐ Matthew 7-9
☐ Matt. 10-12
☐ Matt. 13-15
☐ Matt. 16-18
☐ Matt. 19-21
☐ Matt. 22-24
☐ Matt. 25-26
☐ Matt. 27-28
☐ Mark 1-3
☐ Mark 4-5
☐ Mark 6-8
☐ Mark 9-11
☐ Mark 12-14
☐ Mark 15-16
☐ Luke 1-2
☐ Luke 3-5
☐ Luke 6-7
☐ Luke 8-9
☐ Luke 10-11
☐ Luke 12-14
☐ Luke 15-17
☐ Luke 18-20
☐ Luke 21-22
☐ Luke 23-24
☐ John 1-3
☐ John 4-5
☐ John 6-7
☐ John 8-10
☐ John 11-12
☐ John 13-15
☐ John 16-18
☐ John 19-21
☐ Acts 1-3
☐ Acts 4-6
☐ Acts 7-8
☐ Acts 9-11
☐ Acts 12-15
☐ Acts 16-18
☐ Acts 19-21
☐ Acts 22-24
☐ Acts 25-26
☐ Acts 27-28
☐ Romans 1-3

☐ Romans 4-6
☐ Romans 7-9
☐ Romans 10-12
☐ Romans 13-16
☐ 1 Cor. 1-4
☐ 1 Cor. 5-9
☐ 1 Cor. 10-12
☐ 1 Cor. 13-16
☐ 2 Cor. 1-4
☐ 2 Cor. 5-8
☐ 2 Cor. 9-13
☐ Galatians 1-3
☐ Galatians 4-6
☐ Ephesians 1-3
☐ Ephesians 4-6
☐ Phil. 1-4
☐ Colossians 1-4
☐ 1 Thes. 1-3
☐ 1 Thes. 4-5
☐ 2 Thes. 1-3
☐ 1 Timothy 1-3
☐ 1 Timothy 4-6
☐ 2 Timothy 1-4
☐ Titus 1-3
☐ Philemon
☐ Hebrews 1
☐ Hebrews 2-4
☐ Hebrews 5-7
☐ Hebrews 8-10
☐ Hebrews 11-13
☐ James 1-3
☐ James 4-5
☐ 1 Peter 1-3
☐ 1 Peter 4-5
☐ 2 Peter 1-3
☐ 1 John 1-3
☐ 1 John 4-5
☐ 2 Jn, 3 Jn, Jude
☐ Revelation 1-3
☐ Revelation 4-6
☐ Revelation 7-9
☐ Rev. 10-12
☐ Rev. 13-15
☐ Rev. 16-18
☐ Rev. 19-22

# four times in one year

# Bible reading schedule

**Read through the Bible in one year! As you complete each daily reading, simply place a check in the appropriate box.**

- ☐ 1 Genesis 1-3
- ☐ 2 Genesis 4:1-6:8
- ☐ 3 Genesis 6:9-9:29
- ☐ 4 Genesis 10-11
- ☐ 5 Genesis 12-14
- ☐ 6 Genesis 15-17
- ☐ 7 Genesis 18-19
- ☐ 8 Genesis 20-22
- ☐ 9 Genesis 23-24
- ☐ 10 Genesis 25-26
- ☐ 11 Genesis 27-28
- ☐ 12 Genesis 29-30
- ☐ 13 Genesis 31-32
- ☐ 14 Genesis 33-35
- ☐ 15 Genesis 36-37
- ☐ 16 Genesis 38-40
- ☐ 17 Genesis 41-42
- ☐ 18 Genesis 43-45
- ☐ 19 Genesis 46-47
- ☐ 20 Genesis 48-50
- ☐ 21 Job 1-3
- ☐ 22 Job 4-7
- ☐ 23 Job 8-11
- ☐ 24 Job 12-15
- ☐ 25 Job 16-19
- ☐ 26 Job 20-22
- ☐ 27 Job 23-28
- ☐ 28 Job 29-31
- ☐ 29 Job 32-34
- ☐ 30 Job 35-37
- ☐ 31 Job 38-42
- ☐ 32 Exodus 1-4
- ☐ 33 Exodus 5-8
- ☐ 34 Exodus 9-11
- ☐ 35 Exodus 12-13
- ☐ 36 Exodus 14-15
- ☐ 37 Exodus 16-18
- ☐ 38 Exodus 19-21
- ☐ 39 Exodus 22-24
- ☐ 40 Exodus 25-27
- ☐ 41 Exodus 28-29
- ☐ 42 Exodus 30-31
- ☐ 43 Exodus 32-34
- ☐ 44 Exodus 35-36
- ☐ 45 Exodus 37-38
- ☐ 46 Exodus 39-40
- ☐ 47 Leviticus 1:1-5:13
- ☐ 48 Leviticus 5:14-7:38
- ☐ 49 Leviticus 8-10
- ☐ 50 Leviticus 11-12
- ☐ 51 Leviticus 13-14
- ☐ 52 Leviticus 15-17
- ☐ 53 Leviticus 18-20
- ☐ 54 Leviticus 21-23
- ☐ 55 Leviticus 24-25
- ☐ 56 Leviticus 26-27
- ☐ 57 Numbers 1-2
- ☐ 58 Numbers 3-4
- ☐ 59 Numbers 5-6
- ☐ 60 Numbers 7
- ☐ 61 Numbers 8-10
- ☐ 62 Numbers 11-13
- ☐ 63 Numbers 14-15
- ☐ 64 Numbers 16-18
- ☐ 65 Numbers 19-21
- ☐ 66 Numbers 22-24
- ☐ 67 Numbers 25-26
- ☐ 68 Numbers 27-29
- ☐ 69 Numbers 30-31
- ☐ 70 Numbers 32-33
- ☐ 71 Numbers 34-36
- ☐ 72 Deuteronomy 1-2
- ☐ 73 Deuteronomy 3-4
- ☐ 74 Deuteronomy 5-7
- ☐ 75 Deuteronomy 8-10
- ☐ 76 Deuteronomy 11-13
- ☐ 77 Deuteronomy 14-17
- ☐ 78 Deuteronomy 18-21
- ☐ 79 Deuteronomy 22-25
- ☐ 80 Deuteronomy 26-28
- ☐ 81 Deuteronomy 29:1-31:29
- ☐ 82 Deuteronomy 31:30-34:12
- ☐ 83 Joshua 1-4
- ☐ 84 Joshua 5-8
- ☐ 85 Joshua 9-11
- ☐ 86 Joshua 12-14
- ☐ 87 Joshua 15-17
- ☐ 88 Joshua 18-19
- ☐ 89 Joshua 20-22
- ☐ 90 Joshua 23 - Judges 1
- ☐ 91 Judges 2-5
- ☐ 92 Judges 6-8
- ☐ 93 Judges 9
- ☐ 94 Judges 10-12
- ☐ 95 Judges 13-16
- ☐ 96 Judges 17-19
- ☐ 97 Judges 20-21
- ☐ 98 Ruth
- ☐ 99 1 Samuel 1-3
- ☐ 100 1 Samuel 4-7
- ☐ 101 1 Samuel 8-10
- ☐ 102 1 Samuel 11-13
- ☐ 103 1 Samuel 14-15
- ☐ 104 1 Samuel 16-17

# Bible reading schedule

## Day 105-199

- [ ] 105 1 Samuel 18-19; Psalm 59
- [ ] 106 1 Samuel 20-21; Psalm 56; 34
- [ ] 107 1 Samuel 22-23; 1 Chronicles 12:8-18; Psalm 52; 54; 63; 142
- [ ] 108 1 Samuel 24; Psalm 57; 1 Samuel 25
- [ ] 109 1 Samuel 26-29; 1 Chronicles 12:1-7, 19-22
- [ ] 110 1 Samuel 30-31; 1 Chronicles 10; 2 Samuel 1
- [ ] 111 2 Samuel 2-4
- [ ] 112 2 Samuel 5:1-6:11; 1 Chronicles 11:1-9; 2:23-40; 13:1-14:17
- [ ] 113 2 Samuel 22; Psalm 18
- [ ] 114 1 Chronicles 15-16; 2 Samuel 6:12-23; Psalm 96
- [ ] 115 Psalm 105; 2 Samuel 7; 1 Chronicles 17
- [ ] 116 2 Samuel 8-10; 1 Chronicles 18-19; Psalm 60
- [ ] 117 2 Samuel 11-12; 1 Chronicles 20:1-3; Psalm 51
- [ ] 118 2 Samuel 13-14
- [ ] 119 2 Samuel 15-17
- [ ] 120 Psalm 3; 2 Samuel 18-19
- [ ] 121 2 Samuel 20-21; 23:8-23; 1 Chronicles 20:4-8; 11:10-25
- [ ] 122 2 Samuel 23:24-24:25;
- [ ] 123 1 Chronicles 11:26-47; 21:1-30, 1 Chronicles 22-24
- [ ] 124 Psalm 30; 1 Chronicles 25-26
- [ ] 125 1 Chronicles 27-29
- [ ] 126 Psalms 5-7; 10; 11; 13; 17
- [ ] 127 Psalms 23; 26; 28; 31; 35
- [ ] 128 Psalms 41; 43; 46; 55; 61; 62; 64
- [ ] 129 Psalms 69-71; 77
- [ ] 130 Psalms 83; 86; 88; 91; 95
- [ ] 131 Psalms 108-9; 120-21; 140; 143-44
- [ ] 132 Psalms 1; 14-15; 36-37; 39
- [ ] 133 Psalms 40; 49-50; 73
- [ ] 134 Psalms 76; 82; 84; 90; 92; 112; 115
- [ ] 135 Psalms 8-9; 16; 19; 21; 24; 29
- [ ] 136 Psalms 33; 65-68
- [ ] 137 Psalms 75; 93-94; 97-100
- [ ] 138 Psalms 103-4; 113-14; 117
- [ ] 139 Psalm 119:1-88
- [ ] 140 Psalm 119:89-176
- [ ] 141 Psalms 122; 124; 133-36
- [ ] 142 Psalms 138-39; 145; 148; 150
- [ ] 143 Psalms 4; 12; 20; 25; 32; 38
- [ ] 144 Psalms 42; 53; 58; 81; 101; 111; 130-31;141;146
- [ ] 145 Psalms 2; 22; 27
- [ ] 146 Psalms 45; 47-48; 87; 110
- [ ] 147 1 Kings 1:1-2:12; 2 Samuel 23:1-7
- [ ] 148 1 Kings 2:13-3:28; 2 Chronicles 1:1-13
- [ ] 149 1 Kings 5-6; 2 Chronicles 2-3
- [ ] 150 1 Kings 7; 2 Chronicles 4
- [ ] 151 1 Kings 8; 2 Chronicles 5:1-7:10
- [ ] 152 1 Kings 9:1-10:13; 2 Chronicles 7:11-9:12
- [ ] 153 1 Kings 4; 10:14-29; 2 Chronicles 1:14-17; 9:13-28; Psalm 72
- [ ] 154 Proverbs 1-3
- [ ] 155 Proverbs 4-6
- [ ] 156 Proverbs 7-9
- [ ] 157 Proverbs 10-12
- [ ] 158 Proverbs 13-15
- [ ] 159 Proverbs 16-18
- [ ] 160 Proverbs 19-21
- [ ] 161 Proverbs 22-24
- [ ] 162 Proverbs 25-27
- [ ] 163 Proverbs 28-29
- [ ] 164 Proverbs 30-31; Psalm 127
- [ ] 165 Song of Solomon
- [ ] 166 1 Kings 11:1-40; Ecclesiastes 1-2
- [ ] 167 Ecclesiastes 3-7
- [ ] 168 Ecclesiastes 8-12; 1 Kings 11:41-43; 2 Chronicles 9:29-31
- [ ] 169 1 Kings 12; 2 Chronicles 10:1-11:17
- [ ] 170 1 Kings 13-14; 2 Chronicles 11:18-12:16
- [ ] 171 1 Kings 15:1-24; 2 Chronicles 13-16
- [ ] 172 1 Kings 15:25-16:34; 2 Chronicles 17; 1 Kings 17
- [ ] 173 1 Kings 18-19
- [ ] 174 1 Kings 20-21
- [ ] 175 1 Kings 22:1-40; 2 Chronicles 18
- [ ] 176 1 Kings 22:41-53; 2 Kings 1; 2 Chronicles 19:1-21:3
- [ ] 177 2 Kings 2-4
- [ ] 178 2 Kings 5-7
- [ ] 179 2 Kings 8-9; 2 Chronicles 21:4-22:9
- [ ] 180 2 Kings 10-11; 2 Chronicles 22:10-23:21
- [ ] 181 Joel
- [ ] 182 2 Kings 12-13; 2 Chronicles 24
- [ ] 183 2 Kings 14; 2 Chronicles 25; Jonah
- [ ] 184 Hosea 1-7
- [ ] 185 Hosea 8-14
- [ ] 186 2 Kings 15:1-7; 2 Chronicles 26; Amos 1-4
- [ ] 187 Amos 5-9; 2 Kings 15:8-18
- [ ] 188 Isaiah 1-4
- [ ] 189 2 Kings 15:19-38; 2 Chronicles 27; Isaiah 5-6
- [ ] 190 Micah
- [ ] 191 2 Kings 16; 2 Chronicles 28; Isaiah 7-8
- [ ] 192 Isaiah 9-12
- [ ] 193 Isaiah 13-16
- [ ] 194 Isaiah 17-22
- [ ] 195 Isaiah 23-27
- [ ] 196 Isaiah 28-30
- [ ] 197 Isaiah 31-35
- [ ] 198 2 Kings 18:1-8; 2 Chronicles 29-31
- [ ] 199 2 Kings 17; 18:9-37; 2 Chronicles 32:1-19; Isaiah 36

# Bible reading schedule

## Day 200-288

- ☐ 200 2 Kings 19; 2 Chronicles 32:20-23; Isaiah 37
- ☐ 201 2 Kings 20; 2 Chronicles 32:24-33; Isaiah 38-39
- ☐ 202 2 Kings 21:1-18; 2 Chronicles 33:1-20; Isaiah 40
- ☐ 203 Isaiah 41-43
- ☐ 204 Isaiah 44-47
- ☐ 205 Isaiah 48-51
- ☐ 206 Isaiah 52-57
- ☐ 207 Isaiah 58-62
- ☐ 208 Isaiah 63-66
- ☐ 209 2 Kings 21:19-26; 2 Chronicles 33:21-34:7; Zephaniah
- ☐ 210 Jeremiah 1-3
- ☐ 211 Jeremiah 4-6
- ☐ 212 Jeremiah 7-9
- ☐ 213 Jeremiah 10-13
- ☐ 214 Jeremiah 14-16
- ☐ 215 Jeremiah 17-20
- ☐ 216 2 Kings 22:1-23:28; 2 Chronicles 34:8-35:19
- ☐ 217 Nahum; 2 Kings 23:29-37;
- ☐ 2 Chronicles 35:20-36:5; Jeremiah 22:10-17
- ☐ 218 Jeremiah 26; Habakkuk
- ☐ 219 Jeremiah 46-47; 2 Kings 24:1-4, 7; 2 Chronicles 36:6-7; Jeremiah 25, 35
- ☐ 220 Jeremiah 36, 45, 48
- ☐ 221 Jeremiah 49:1-33; Daniel 1-2
- ☐ 222 Jeremiah 22:18-30; 2 Kings 24:5-20; 2 Chronicles 36:8-12; Jeremiah 37:1-2; 52:1-3; 24; 29
- ☐ 223 Jeremiah 27-28, 23
- ☐ 224 Jeremiah 50-51
- ☐ 225 Jeremiah 49:34-39; 34:1-22; Ezekiel 1-3
- ☐ 226 Ezekiel 4-7
- ☐ 227 Ezekiel 8-11
- ☐ 228 Ezekiel 12-14
- ☐ 229 Ezekiel 15-17
- ☐ 230 Ezekiel 18-20
- ☐ 231 Ezekiel 21-23
- ☐ 232 2 Kings 25:1; 2 Chronicles 36:13-16; Jeremiah 39:1; 52:4; Ezekiel 24; Jeremiah 21:1-22:9; 32:1-44
- ☐ 233 Jeremiah 30-31, 33
- ☐ 234 Ezekiel 25; 29:1-16; 30; 31
- ☐ 235 Ezekiel 26-28
- ☐ 236 Jeremiah 37:3-39:10; 52:5-30; 2 Kings 25:2-21; 2 Chronicles 36:17-21
- ☐ 237 2 Kings 25:22; Jeremiah 39:11-40:6; Lamentations 1-3
- ☐ 238 Lamentations 4-5; Obadiah
- ☐ 239 Jeremiah 40:7-44:30; 2 Kings 25:23-26
- ☐ 240 Ezekiel 33:21-36:38
- ☐ 241 Ezekiel 37-39
- ☐ 242 Ezekiel 32:1-33:20; Daniel 3
- ☐ 243 Ezekiel 40-42
- ☐ 244 Ezekiel 43-45
- ☐ 245 Ezekiel 46-48
- ☐ 246 Ezekiel 29:17-21; Daniel 4; Jeremiah 52:31-34; 2 Kings 25:27-30; Psalm 44
- ☐ 247 Psalms 74; 79-80; 89
- ☐ 248 Psalms 85; 102; 106; 123; 137
- ☐ 249 Daniel 7-8; 5
- ☐ 250 Daniel 9; 6
- ☐ 251 2 Chronicles 36:22-23; Ezra 1:1-4:5
- ☐ 252 Daniel 10-12
- ☐ 253 Ezra 4:6-6:13; Haggai
- ☐ 254 Zechariah 1-6
- ☐ 255 Zechariah 7-8; Ezra 6:14-22; Psalm 78
- ☐ 256 Psalms 107; 116; 118
- ☐ 257 Psalms 125-26; 128-29; 132; 147; 149
- ☐ 258 Zechariah 9-14
- ☐ 259 Esther 1-4
- ☐ 260 Esther 5-10
- ☐ 261 Ezra 7-8
- ☐ 262 Ezra 9-10
- ☐ 263 Nehemiah 1-5
- ☐ 264 Nehemiah 6-7
- ☐ 265 Nehemiah 8-10
- ☐ 266 Nehemiah 11-13
- ☐ 267 Malachi
- ☐ 268 1 Chronicles 1-2
- ☐ 269 1 Chronicles 3-5
- ☐ 270 1 Chronicles 6
- ☐ 271 1 Chronicles 7:1-8:27
- ☐ 272 1 Chronicles 8:28-9:44
- ☐ 273 John 1:1-18; Mark 1:1; Luke 1:1-4; 3:23-38; Matthew 1:1-17
- ☐ 274 Luke 1:5-80
- ☐ 275 Matthew 1:18-2:23; Luke 2
- ☐ 276 Matthew 3:1-4:11; Mark 1:2-13; Luke 3:1-23; 4:1-13; John 1:19-34
- ☐ 277 John 1:35-3:36
- ☐ 278 John 4; Matthew 4:12-17; Mark 1:14-15; Luke 4:14-30
- ☐ 279 Mark 1:16-45; Matthew 4:18-25; 8:2-4, 14-17; Luke 4:31-5:16
- ☐ 280 Matthew 9:1-17; Mark 2:1-22; Luke 5:17-39
- ☐ 281 John 5; Matthew 12:1-21; Mark 2:23-3:12; Luke 6:1-11
- ☐ 282 Matthew 5; Mark 3:13-19; Luke 6:12-36
- ☐ 283 Matthew 6-7; Luke 6:37-49
- ☐ 284 Luke 7; Matthew 8:1, 5-13; 11:2-30
- ☐ 285 Matthew 12:22-50; Mark 3:20-35; Luke 8:1-21
- ☐ 286 Mark 4:1-34; Matthew 13:1-53
- ☐ 287 Mark 4:35-5:43; Matthew 8:18, 23-34; 9:18-34; Luke 8:22-56
- ☐ 288 Mark 6:1-30; Matthew 13:54-58; 9:35-11:1; 14:1-12; Luke 9:1-10

# Bible reading schedule

**Day 289-365**

- ☐ 289 Matthew 14:13-36; Mark 6:31-56; Luke 9:11-17; John 6:1-21
- ☐ 290 John 6:22-7:1; Matthew 15:1-20; Mark 7:1-23
- ☐ 291 Matthew 15:21-16:20; Mark 7:24-8:30; Luke 9:18-21
- ☐ 292 Matthew 16:21-17:27; Mark 8:31-9:32; Luke 9:22-45
- ☐ 293 Matthew 18; 8:19-22; Mark 9:33-50; Luke 9:46-62; John 7:2-10
- ☐ 294 John 7:11-8:59
- ☐ 295 Luke 10:1-11:36
- ☐ 296 Luke 11:37-13:21
- ☐ 297 John 9-10
- ☐ 298 Luke 13:22-15:32
- ☐ 299 Luke 16:1-17:10; John 11:1-54
- ☐ 300 Luke 17:11-18:17; Matthew 19:1-15; Mark 10:1-16
- ☐ 301 Matthew 19:16-20:28; Mark 10:17-45; Luke 18:18-34
- ☐ 302 Matthew 20:29-34; 26:6-13; Mark 10:46-52; 14:3-9; Luke 18:35-19:28; John 11:55-12:11
- ☐ 303 Matthew 21:1-22; Mark 11:1-26; Luke 19:29-48; John 12:12-50
- ☐ 304 Matthew 21:23-22:14; Mark 11:27-12:12; Luke 20:1-19
- ☐ 305 Matthew 22:15-46; Mark 12:13-37; Luke 20:20-44
- ☐ 306 Matthew 23; Mark 12:38-44; Luke 20:45-21:4
- ☐ 307 Matthew 24:1-31; Mark 13:1-27; Luke 21:5-27
- ☐ 308 Matthew 24:32-26:5, 14-16; Mark 13:28-14:2, 10-11; Luke 21:28-22:6
- ☐ 309 Matthew 26:17-29; Mark 14:12-25; Luke 22:7-38; John 13
- ☐ 310 John 14-16
- ☐ 311 John 17:1-18:1; Matthew 26:30-46; Mark 14:26-42; Luke 22:39-46
- ☐ 312 Matthew 26:47-75; Mark 14:43-72; Luke 22:47-65; John 18:2-27
- ☐ 313 Matthew 27:1-26; Mark 15:1-15; Luke 22:66-23:25; John 18:28-19:16
- ☐ 314 Matthew 27:27-56; Mark 15:16-41; Luke 23:26-49; John 19:17-30
- ☐ 315 Matthew 27:57-28:8; Mark 15:42-16:8; Luke 23:50-24:12; John 19:31-20:10
- ☐ 316 Matthew 28:9-20; Mark 16:9-20; Luke 24:13-53; John 20:11-21:25
- ☐ 317 Acts 1-2
- ☐ 318 Acts 3-5
- ☐ 319 Acts 6:1-8:1
- ☐ 320 Acts 8:2-9:43
- ☐ 321 Acts 10-11
- ☐ 322 Acts 12-13
- ☐ 323 Acts 14-15
- ☐ 324 Galatians 1-3
- ☐ 325 Galatians 4-6
- ☐ 326 James
- ☐ 327 Acts 16:1-18:11
- ☐ 328 1 Thessalonians
- ☐ 329 2 Thessalonians; Acts 18:12-19:22
- ☐ 330 1 Corinthians 1-4
- ☐ 331 1 Corinthians 5-8
- ☐ 332 1 Corinthians 9-11
- ☐ 333 1 Corinthians 12-14
- ☐ 334 1 Corinthians 15-16
- ☐ 335 Acts 19:23-20:1; 2 Corinthians 1-4
- ☐ 336 2 Corinthians 5-9
- ☐ 337 2 Corinthians 10-13
- ☐ 338 Romans 1-3
- ☐ 339 Romans 4-6
- ☐ 340 Romans 7-8
- ☐ 341 Romans 9-11
- ☐ 342 Romans 12-15
- ☐ 343 Romans 16; Acts 20:2-21:16
- ☐ 344 Acts 21:17-23:35
- ☐ 345 Acts 24-26
- ☐ 346 Acts 27-28
- ☐ 347 Ephesians 1-3
- ☐ 348 Ephesians 4-6
- ☐ 349 Colossians
- ☐ 350 Philippians
- ☐ 351 Philemon; 1 Timothy 1-3
- ☐ 352 1 Timothy 4-6; Titus
- ☐ 353 2 Timothy
- ☐ 354 1 Peter
- ☐ 355 Jude; 2 Peter
- ☐ 356 Hebrews 1:1-5:10
- ☐ 357 Hebrews 5:11-9:28
- ☐ 358 Hebrews 10-11
- ☐ 359 Hebrews 12-13; 2 John; 3 John
- ☐ 360 1 John
- ☐ 361 Revelation 1-3
- ☐ 362 Revelation 4-9
- ☐ 363 Revelation 10-14
- ☐ 364 Revelation 15-18
- ☐ 365 Revelation 19-22

Week 8

The best teeter-totter partners are two who weigh about the same. However, if a second person gets on one end, the two outweigh the other leaving him stuck in the up position. This week we will see how righteous choices outweigh ungodly choices and how they can change the balance of things and benefit our lives.

Prayer Focus for this week:

**Q: The QUESTION - What is the writer saying?**

**A: The APPLICATION- How can I apply this to my life?**

Sunday Psalm 1:1-6

Q:

A:

Digging DEEPER

Most of us do not want to be compared to a brother or sister especially if they excel at something we are not very good at. Today's psalm compares two people. One is described as blessed because he has made righteous choices. The other is called ungodly because he has chosen just the opposite. The righteous do not seek counsel from the ungodly, sinners, or the scornful. They look instead to God's Word (v. 2) which gives life and causes growth like the tree by the river that bears fruit and prospers (v. 3). By contrast, the ungodly become like wheat chaff (v. 4) and perish from their choices (v. 6).

***When the fruit of your choices is fully grown, will you prosper like the righteous or perish like the ungodly?***

Life stEP

Monday Psalm 2:1-12

Q:

A:

**Digging DEEPER** We all look forward to the time when we are independent from mom and dad and able to make our own decisions without following their rules. The same is true of the world. When it comes to following God's guidelines, they are not interested in God telling them how to live their lives. In Psalm 2, God the Father is speaking to God the Son. He tells Him that He has power and authority over the nations of the world, and He will bring them into compliance or they will be destroyed (vv. 6-9). God the Son then encourages the nations to be wise, to serve Him, and respect Him rather than to rebel and know His wrath.

*List two areas in your life where you have followed your own rules and have gotten into trouble. List two areas where you have allowed God to guide you.*

Tuesday Psalm 3:1-8

Q:

A:

**Digging DEEPER** We each know someone who has feared for his life. Whether he leaves town or hides, the danger is real. David wrote Psalm 3 after running from his son who sought to kill him. David prayed to God and remembered that God heard his prayer and protected him from his enemy. David believed that God would protect him so that he was able to rest his heart and mind. He actually fell asleep. The Lord is our Shield and the One who lifts our head in encouragement. When all else fails the Lord sustains us (v. 5).

*When you are up against one who threatens you, read Psalm 3. Remember God is your Protector and He will give you the strength to overcome in times of danger. What can you trust Him for today?*

Life stEP

Week 1

Wednesday Psalm 4:1-8

Every four years the world sends her best athletes to compete in the Olympics. Men and women train and prepare for years just to be in these games. Athletes who represent their country are expected to be in much better physical shape than the people back home sitting on the couch watching them on TV. God has set apart those who are godly for Himself (v. 3) and He expects us to live a life of sacrifice and to put our trust in Him (v. 5). Just as nations look to their athletes as an encouragement, we as believers are to show the light of God through the gladness of our hearts (v. 7) to those who wonder if there is still any good left in this world(v. 6). This is best done when we show God's peace in our lives.

***List at least two people you can encourage this week.***

Thursday Psalm 5:1-12

Contrast and comparison – we are bombarded with it every day in advertisements, commercials, and people trying to sell us stuff that will make us more like the people in their ad. Psalm 5 is a comparison between the righteous and the wicked. The Lord hears the voice of the righteous (v. 3) but hates all workers of iniquity (v. 5). While the righteous desire to be led by the Lord (v. 8), the ungodly rebel against Him (v. 10). Those who put their trust in God rejoice and are joyful (v. 11), and God blesses the righteous (v. 12).

***List two ways that you are the same as your unsaved friends – two things that you would like to change. Which verses in today's passage can help?***

Friday Psalm 6:1-10

Q:

A:

**Digging DEEPER** Each of us has known someone who has been under the influence of drugs or alcohol and has seen the effects on his life. The remedy for such addictions is often extreme but very necessary if the individual is going to be saved. Sin takes us further than we wanted to go, keeps us longer than we want to stay, and costs us more than we want to pay. The Biblical cure for our sin begins with repentance from a broken heart. David understood this and wrote four psalms declaring his regret for the sins he committed against God. Psalm 6, 32, 38, and 51 are expressions of someone willing to admit his sin against a holy God.

***Spend time in prayer: be honest with God about sins of which you need to repent. Then do it!***

Saturday Psalm 7:1-8

Q:

A:

**Digging DEEPER** Picture yourself in a courtroom on trial for something of which you are innocent. The prosecution rests. Now it is time for your defense attorney to call his witness. He stands up and calls God to the witness stand. Can you think of a better witness? There is no one better to have standing on our side to speak for us. David knew that, and in today's passage he calls on God to save him and deliver him (v. 1), and to rise up for him in judgment against his enemies. David prayed and asked God to judge him according to his righteousness and integrity (which was in contrast to the ungodly enemies of Israel).

***Name a time when you were falsely accused but later proven innocent. When God stands with the righteous, we have the strength to stand alone.***

Week 2

When a father holds His newborn baby for the first time, he has absolute power and control over that child. He is strong enough to destroy the child and yet he uses his strength to guard and protect his baby. God who has created all things is strong enough to guard and protect us from the schemes of the wicked.

Prayer Focus for this week:

**Q: The QUESTION - What is the writer saying?**

**A: The APPLICATION- How can I apply this to my life?**

Sunday Psalm 7:9-17

Q:

A:

Digging DEEPER

We are each familiar with warnings that we see every day. Flashing lights, barricades, and signs warn us to be cautious or take a different route. In today's passage, David gives three points or signs to his readers. First, God establishes the just and saves the upright but is angry with the wicked every day. Second, God has sharpened His sword and bent his bow in preparation to deal justly with the wicked. Third, David describes the wicked (vv. 14 -16) as a warning. He warns the righteous to avoid that path in life and warns the wicked so they know the kind of behavior God will judge. David's desire is that wickedness ends (v. 9), either through the changed heart of the wicked or the sustained righteousness of the just.

***List three ways you can maintain a pattern of doing right in your life.***

Life stEP

Monday Psalm 8:1-9

Q:

A:

**Digging Deeper** Each of us has responsibilities, whether it is school work, jobs, or working around the house. In Psalm 8, we are reminded that God gave a huge responsibility to man (Adam) when He gave him dominion (rule) over all the earth. God gave Adam a great privilege when He put him in charge. However, Adam gave it up to Satan when he gave into temptation and ate the forbidden fruit. Rule over the earth will be regained by Christ when all things are put under His feet (v. 6) or under His reign again at His second coming. God is always in control of what Satan is allowed to do. For now, Satan is allowed to rule over the earth. We can be encouraged with the fact that God is really in ultimate control.

*List three areas where you can see that God governs Satan's rule on earth.*

Tuesday Psalm 9:1-10

Q:

A:

**Digging Deeper** We always have something for which to be thankful. There is always a bright spot even when life is a mess. David looks to the marvelous works of God. The Lord will endure forever (v. 7). He is our refuge (v. 9). He has not forsaken those who seek Him (v. 10). When we look at the condition of the world and even our own country, it is easy to be frustrated and even a little scared at what we see. Psalm 9 helps us with perspective as David gives us a look at life from God's viewpoint rather than the viewpoint we hear or read in the news. The fact that God is our refuge in time of trouble encourages us not to give up. God has not forsaken us (v. 10). We should have courage in times of trouble.

*List two times when God's faithfulness gave you the courage not to quit.*

Wednesday Psalm 9:11-20

Q:

A:

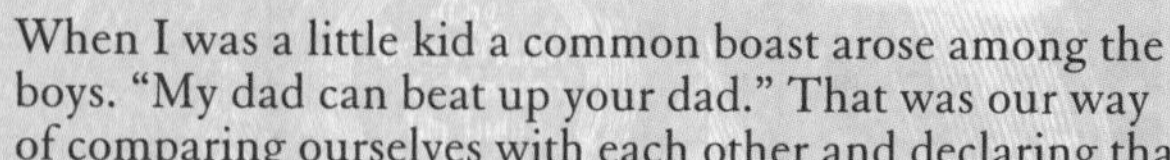

Digging Deeper

When I was a little kid a common boast arose among the boys. "My dad can beat up your dad." That was our way of comparing ourselves with each other and declaring that we, and our dad, were tougher than anyone else. David does that very thing in today's passage when describing his heavenly Father. David states that the Lord is known by the judgment He executes (v. 16). He asks God to judge the nations and not allow men to prevail (v. 19). David is careful to remind his readers that God does not forget the cry of the humble (v. 12). Therefore, we can boldly ask for God's mercy (v. 13). The difference between God and any of our dads is that God really does have the strength to judge the nations.

***Read 1 Samuel 17:29-47 and write why David trusted in God so much. Then name something for which you can trust God.***

Life stEP

Thursday Psalm 10:1-11

Q:

A:

Digging Deeper

It is often said that there is never a police officer around when you need one. In Psalm 10 David wonders why God seems to be standing far off and hiding during his times of trouble (v. 1). The wicked persecute the poor. They are boastful and proud. They do not seek God and they do not even think about Him. The wicked do not even consider God. They curse and are deceitful; trouble and iniquity are under their tongue (v. 7). The situation seems so bad that David believes God has forgotten him and is hiding His face from man's wickedness. God does judge the wicked and they will not get away with their sin. But God is also patient and merciful, and acts in His timing, not ours.

***List three reasons why the wicked will not get away with their sin. If God sees and judges sin, are there things in my life that need to be dealt with?***

Life stEP

Friday Psalm 10:12-18

Q:

A:

Digging DEEPER Many things in life are not guaranteed. We don't know if we will live another day or if we will lose all we have in an accident or natural disaster. We have no assurance that our life will go along with no problems because God does not promise a trouble-free life. However, there are certain things that do not change – things that we can always depend on. David mentions two characteristics about God we can count on. First, the Lord is King forever and ever (v. 16). We all have seen what life is like when man is in charge and it is encouraging to know God is King. Second, He has heard the desire of the humble (v. 17). God knows me. He hears me because He is waiting and listening for me to call on Him.

***Who do you know who needs to hear these encouraging words? Tell them.*** Life stEP

Saturday Psalm 11:1-7

Q:

A:

Digging DEEPER If an enemy was attacking your town or city and they were only an hour from your home, you would only have time to grab a few things as you fled for your life. This happens in many nations around the world where people have had to run for their lives and some are even killed. David is saying that he is not going to run (v. 1). He does not fear the wicked because he has put his trust in the Lord. The Lord is in His holy temple; His throne is in heaven. He sees everything and is going to rain coals down upon the wicked (v. 6). There is peace in the heart of the person who knows and understands that God is in control and that He loves the righteous (v. 7).

***List three things about God, which cause your heart to be at peace.***

Week 3

Have you ever felt left out or left behind? It's not a very comfortable feeling, but when everything is worked out there's a feeling or sensation of acceptance. In this week's passages, you will learn that even though it seems like God is slow in responding, you are still considered by Him to be a V.I.P. (*Very Important Person*).

Prayer Focus for this week:

**Q: The QUESTION - What is the writer saying?**
**A: The APPLICATION- How can I apply this to my life?**

Sunday Psalm 12:1-8

Q:

A:

Digging DEEPER

Talk is cheap and flattery is insincere but we hear it every day from people who want something from us or want us to believe they really like us. The truth is that all they care about is themselves. Verse 4 reminds us of the pride of the ungodly who believe that no one is lord over them and they will be able to *prevail* because of the flattery and deceit of their own tongue. We should be aware of that prideful attitude and take inventory of our own heart so we do not fall into the same trap. The solution for the believer is obvious in verses 6-7 where David reminds us that the words of the Lord are *pure words* and the Lord shall *keep them* and *preserve them*. The Word of God rules over the prideful boasts of the ungodly.

***List two ways your tongue has gotten you in trouble. Confess these if needed and ask the Lord to help you with your speech.***

Monday Psalm 13:1-6

Q:

A:

**Digging Deeper** At times, it seemed to David that the Lord had forgotten him (v. 1). During those times, he would counsel with himself and try to solve his problems using his own ability. This brought nothing but sorrow (v. 2). Next, he pled with God begging for enlightenment (v. 3). Then he tried reasoning with God, explaining that the enemy would be the one to benefit by his (David's) death (v. 4). The Lord answered by supplying David with ample faith to trust (v. 5; Romans 12:3). In spite of terrible circumstances, David rejoiced in the salvation God had promised. David's faith produced singing and this Psalm for us.

***List two things that cause you repeated frustration or give you cause to doubt God. What does this Psalm offer to help you replace that doubt?*** **Life stEP**

Tuesday Psalm 14:1-7

Q:

A:

**Digging Deeper** Many centuries ago, some believed the earth was flat and the sun revolved around the earth. If anyone still believed these fallacies today, he would be considered a fool. Yet with all the evidence we have of God's existence, there are still people who say there is no God. Verses 1 and 3 give a clear description of the people who live like there is no God. They are corrupt, have done abominable works, and none of them does good (v. 1). David paints the same picture of these *fools* in verse 3, where he says they have *turned aside* (become corrupt) and none of them does good. In our lives, when we set ourselves up as god, we become fools and naturally behave as fools.

***List three areas in your life that you know God wants you to change but still you remain stubborn.*** **Life stEP**

Week 3

Wednesday Psalm 15:1-5

Walk, works, and words are three ways we use to evaluate a person. We determine whether or not he can be trusted or whether we want him as a friend. Verses 2-4 give us a clear image of the righteous person. He is someone who walks uprightly, works righteousness, and speaks the truth in his heart. The person in verse 3 treats his neighbor with love and respect. He reflects the righteous life God expects of us. Verse 4 emphasizes the importance of keeping our word even when it costs us something. When we practice these things in real life, people get to see the reality of the God we know and will want to seek Him for answers in their own life.

***Since people see Christ through you, what needs to be cleared away so they have a better view of who He is?***

Thursday Psalm 16:1-11

Psalm 16 is another reminder that God orchestrates all of history and knows the beginning from the end (Isaiah 46:8-10). Verses 8-11reference Christ's future ministry on the earth (to which Peter referred in Acts 2:25-28). God spoke of His Son through David many centuries before Christ's birth to remind us that He is the One who plans history and brings it to pass. David is overwhelmed with all that God is and for His provision for him throughout his life. David understood that what he had was not as important as who he was, and who he was came from the Lord (v. 9).

***List four things that are different about you because you belong to the Lord.***

Life stEP

Friday Psalm 17:1-7

Q:

A:

**Digging DEEPER** Remember when you were a kid and got lost in the mall or on a hiking trip? You couldn't find your parents for what seemed like *forever.* In Psalm 17, David is discouraged with life and needs the Lord he has come to know, love, and depend on. David knew that God, much like our own parents, heard him when he called. He asked his Lord to uphold his steps so that he would not slip or stumble (v. 5). David did not turn to friends, entertainment, or take a vacation; he relied on God to restore his soul and looked to Him for His protection. Remembering the blessings of love and preservation he had enjoyed so much from his Lord, David wrote verse 7.

**Life stEP** *Read verse 7 again and make a list of the evidences of God's love in your life.*

Saturday Psalm 17:8-15

Q:

A:

**Digging DEEPER** Teacher's pet is not a label that most of us want, but we do like it when we get special privileges from our teacher, boss, or parents. David understands that he is important to God. He knows that God considers him the *apple of His eye* (someone who is dear and needs safeguarding). David believes what so many of us doubt – that God is the One who delivers us from the wicked. We believe that we are the one who has the power to deliver ourselves from the wicked, or from uncomfortable circumstances, or from fearful situations by our own power. David was satisfied with his Lord (v. 15) and he encourages us to be satisfied with Him also.

*Take a couple of minutes in prayer thanking the Lord for all He has done for you.*

Week 4

If we are going into battle with an enemy, each of us wants the biggest and best on our side. David tells his readers repeatedly of God's strength to defeat the enemy and deliver him from destruction. Because of God's strength, David has courage to serve His Lord and give Him his life.

Prayer Focus for this week:

**Q: The QUESTION - What is the writer saying?**
**A: The APPLICATION- How can I apply this to my life?**

Sunday Psalm 18:1-12

Q:

A:

Digging DEEPER

When someone is rescued from a fire, drowning, or natural disaster, they are grateful to the person who came to their rescue. The scene is often emotional as credit and thanks are given to the one who has saved lives. David gives God credit and praise for deliverance from snares of death and the sorrows of hell (vv. 5-6). Once more David records those characteristics of God that have brought him through so many dangers and threats from the ungodly. In verses 1-2, we have the list of what God means to David. The Lord is his strength, rock, fortress, deliverer, shield, horn of salvation, and stronghold. David concludes that he will be saved from his enemies.

*Talk to your parents and list three occasions when the Lord delivered your family.*

Monday Psalm 18:13-24

Q:

A:

**Digging Deeper** A familiar chorus says, "*My God is so great; so strong and so mighty. There's nothing that my God cannot do.*" Rather than fight each other, we put our trust in the strength of our Father to defeat the father of our enemy. Verses 13-14 record God's response to those who have come up against His servant David. The Lord thundered from heaven, sent hailstones, coals of fire, arrows, and lightning to vanquish, crush, and annihilate the enemy. The Lord not only defeated the enemy but He comforted (v. 18), delivered (v. 19), and rewarded (v. 20) David because he had kept the ways of the Lord and was faithful to God's statutes (God's Word).

***List two ways we should respond to the Lord because He delivers us. List two reasons we often forget to thank the Lord for His deliverance.*** **Life stEP**

Tuesday Psalm 18:25-36

Q:

A:

**Digging Deeper** In today's society, there are only a few who possess courage. Satan uses fear and complacency to keep people from Christ. Then he uses the same strategy to make Christians ineffective for His kingdom. A soldier who hides in the closet or under his bed is of no use in the time of battle. David understood that his courage came from the Lord and he put that bravery to good use in the service of His Lord and King. Notice David's confidence in verse 29. He says that because of God he was able to go up against a troop of the enemy and even leap over a wall. This was David's way of saying that with God, nothing is too difficult and he was speaking from experience.

*Are you willing to show up for "active duty" today? What can you do? What will you do?*

Wednesday Psalm 18:37-50

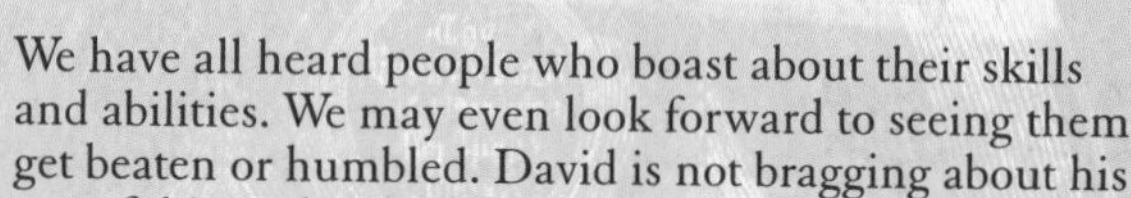

**Digging Deeper**

We have all heard people who boast about their skills and abilities. We may even look forward to seeing them get beaten or humbled. David is not bragging about his greatness in the last part of this psalm; he is bragging on God and all that He has accomplished through David. Notice David gives credit to God. "You have armed me with strength; You have subdued under me the necks of my enemies" (v. 39). "It is God who avenges me. He delivers me from my enemies. You have delivered me from the violent man" (vv. 47-48). It is not boasting to give testimony of God's faithfulness in our lives. It brings glory to God for who He is and what He has done.

***List three reasons we should give God the glory for what He does.***

**Life stEP**

Thursday Psalm 19:1-14

**Digging Deeper**

When we break a law that we did not know about, the police officer will tell us that ignorance is no excuse. We are supposed to know right from wrong so we may avoid the consequences. David wanted to know his errors, faults, and sins. His goal was not to see all that he could get away with but to put his life before the Lord to find what was wrong and what needed adjustment. It is the unbeliever who wants to get away with sin, but that should never be the case for the child of God who loves his Lord. We should ask God (who knows our heart, every thought, and every action) to cleanse us from our sin and keep us from wrongdoing.

***Read verse 14 and list two ways you can make this happen in your life.***

Friday Psalm 20:1-9

Q:

A:

Digging DEEPER

Have you ever seen people gang up on someone they hate? People join forces to defeat a common enemy. The scene for Psalm 20 is set in Jerusalem as King David and his general, Joab, are preparing to face superior enemy forces in battle. The event is thought to be recorded in 2 Samuel 10 and 1 Chronicles 19. The Ammonites joined with the Syrians to overthrow David's rule. They hired thousands of chariots and foot soldiers to fight against David. As was his custom before going into battle, David called his people to worship and sacrifice. Not frightened or discouraged at the overwhelming odds, David simply stated the obvious in verse 7 and His courage increased for battle.

Life stEP

***List two ineffective things people and nations depend on for their success.***

Saturday Psalm 21:1-13

Q:

A:

Digging DEEPER

*Trust me* is a phrase we often hear and yet we have become skeptical because fewer and fewer people are trustworthy these days. Our experience with people may be similar to the cat holding the canary while asking the canary to trust him. Psalm 21 is a good summary to this week of Bible study because David pronounces the blessings and goodness of God on him and his kingship once more. David rejoices that the Lord has dealt with all his enemies and proclaims his trust in God in verse 6. Verse 13 is a fitting end to this week in Psalms. "Be thou exalted, Lord, in thine own strength: so will we sing and praise thy power."

***Read back over this week and think about all God does for us.***

Week 5

**We need to understand that if God is going to help us live our *Christian* lives, we must come to Him in a spirit of humility. Our attitude must honor Him just as Christ did by submitting to God's will when He went to the cross to die for our sin. God resists the proud but allows the humble to do His will.**

Prayer Focus for this week:

**Q: The QUESTION - What is the writer saying?**

**A: The APPLICATION- How can I apply this to my life?**

Sunday Psalm 22:1-11

Q:

A:

Digging DEEPER

Today's Scripture reading points to Christ's death! The fulfillment of this passage is recorded in Matthew 27:39-49 and to some extent in the other three Gospels. Although this was recorded during David's life, it indicated what would happen a thousand years later. For His own purposes, God wanted to record what would transpire a thousand years later in history. Specifically, He is revealing the anguish that our Savior endured while hanging on the cross. Verses 6-11 describe the heart sufferings of Christ because of rejection by His fellow man. The emphasis in these verses is upon the emotional and psychological effects that the cross had on Christ.

***Make a list of the things Christ experienced that also affect us. Select one or two and express your appreciation to Him today.***

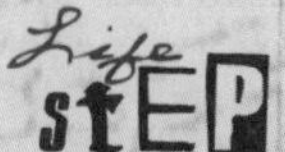

Monday Psalm 22:12-21

Q:

A:

**Digging DEEPER** Most of us are unfamiliar with the cruelty of men on others except through things we see from the news. We never hear about all of the innocent people tortured every day by ungodly men. Crucifixion on the cross was the most horrible form of execution used in Jesus' day. Nevertheless, David graphically described it hundreds of years before it was ever practiced. Even when we concentrate on the physical effects of the crucifixion, we cannot imagine the suffering Christ experienced. This prophecy is an account of a horrible day in history when God the Father allowed His Son to bear the sins of the world on Himself. Yet it ends with God answering and delivering His Son.

***What is the worst thing you have suffered? Now compare them with what Christ endured, then express your thanks to Him for His love and grace.*** **Life stEP**

Tuesday Psalm 22:22-31

Q:

A:

**Digging DEEPER** We are all familiar with war. Whether our country is directly involved or not, we are still affected by it. When the battle is over and the victory is won, there is always a celebration. Here in the last part of this psalm, we see the outcome of Christ's resurrection and His victory over death and the grave. The principle theme of today's Scripture is "praise to the LORD in the coming kingdom." The king will praise Him (v. 22). The descendants of Jacob will praise and glorify Him (v. 23). The Psalmist will praise Him (v. 25). The lowly will praise Him (v. 26). All individuals and all nations shall worship Him because Jesus Christ will rule over all the nations (vv. 27-29).

***Name something for which you will praise the Lord today. Why not praise Him for it right now?***

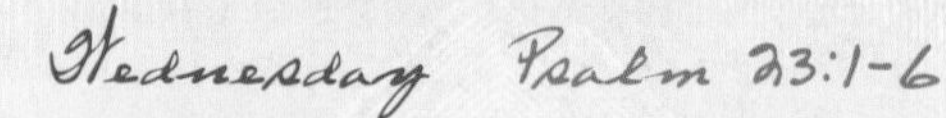


**Digging DEEPER**

It is characteristic of humans to want more than we have. It is also human nature not to be satisfied once we get it. Little children often have the hardest time with contentment because they want everything. Psalm 23 is the perfect picture of the perfect Shepherd who takes perfect care of His sheep. David was a shepherd. He knew first hand what it meant to care for and protect his flock. He uses this to illustrate the way God loves and cares for us. God leads me, restores me, protects me from my enemies, and even cares for my everyday physical needs. We can say that we will fear no evil (v. 4) and that goodness and mercy follow us because of who our Shepherd is.

**Life stEP**

***Tell someone today about the goodness of your Lord and what that goodness means to you.***

Thursday Psalm 24:1-10

**Digging DEEPER**

If I came to your house, I would not go through each room claiming that everything belonged to me nor would I be the one to set the rules of the house. Psalm 24 reminds us that the earth and the entire world along with everything in it belong to the Lord. We are also reminded that we don't make the rules in God's world. Since we will stand before Him one day, we must purify our hearts from sin receiving Him as our Savior. We are told, once again, that all of heaven and earth belong to the Lord strong and mighty. He is the King of glory.

***Find something of yours that you enjoy and give it to someone less fortunate. It all belongs to the Lord anyway; we just take care of it for Him.***

Friday Psalm 25:1-11

Q:

A:

**Digging DEEPER** We have all been let down or disappointed by someone. That is just the way of the human race. When he uses the word *ashamed*, David is not speaking about feelings of guilt, disgrace, or embarrassment. *Ashamed* here means being let down or disappointed because of misplaced trust. David states, for the record, that no person who waits in faith on the Lord is ever ashamed, disappointed, or let down. David is not proud. In verses 4-5, He asks for guidance and instruction to follow God's ways. God teaches the humble person His ways and shows him the path of mercy and truth (v. 10), and pardons his iniquity (sin).

***List three stubborn areas in your life that you find difficult asking for God's guidance. Why not pick one and surrender it to God today?*** **Life stEP**

Saturday Psalm 25:12-22

Q:

A:

**Digging DEEPER** Before a wild horse can be ridden, it must be broken. If it is not, it will not follow the direction the rider wants to take. The same is true of man. Those who fear (respect and honor) the Lord will benefit from His promise or covenant (v. 14). In humbleness, they are willing to let God lead their lives. Many of us go through life with the attitude that *no one is going to tell me what to do.* That approach will get us into big trouble with others someday and certainly with the Lord every day. David asks for mercy in verse 16. Mercy is something we all need from God on a regular basis. God resists the proud but gives grace to the humble (James 4:6).

***Name one thing in your life that you are too proud to give to the Lord. Is it worth missing the blessing of God in your life? Turn it over to God today.***

Week 8

Who are you most thankful for in your life? We all appreciate those who love and provide for us or do things on our behalf. Nevertheless, have you seriously considered all that God has done for you? Paul will teach us this week that we are truly loved and blessed by God through the Lord Jesus Christ.

Prayer Focus for this week:

**Q: The QUESTION - What is the writer saying?**

**A: The APPLICATION- How can I apply this to my life?**

Sunday Ephesians 1:1-6

Q:

A:

Digging DEEPER

Have you ever asked yourself "Who am I?" That is a question we all ask at some point in our lives. At salvation, we become *in Christ* through the forgiveness of our sins, and we become *saints*, meaning to be set apart for God. We must follow that by deciding daily to live out our position (in Christ) with our actions. We may not always act like saints, but that is who we are *in Christ*. Meditate on these things. Paul points out what we as saints have. First, God chose us (v. 4). Second, He adopted us as His children (v. 5). Third, we have "all spiritual blessings…in Christ" (v. 3). Fourth, we can be holy and without blame before Him in love (v. 4).

***Who are you? Are you a saint? Praise God for the four areas listed above. Make a list of what God has done for you lately.***

Life stEP

Monday Ephesians 1:7-14

Q:

A:

**Digging DEEPER** As you read a mystery have you ever gotten frustrated with the author for not revealing enough information? Early in this book (vv. 8-10) Paul tells us that, in God's grace, the believer has the resources necessary to comprehend God's will and purpose. The *inheritance* we have can be read two ways: "We have obtained an inheritance" (Romans 8:17), or "We were made His inheritance" (Hebrews 12:2). Both are true. We are also "sealed with the Holy Spirit" (v. 14). This is a mark of ownership and a pledge from God that our redemption will be completed in heaven.

***Do you understand God's will for your life? Are you sealed with the Holy Spirit? Ask God and a leader to help you understand what you have in Christ.*** **Life stEP**

Tuesday Ephesians 1:15-23

Q:

A:

**Digging DEEPER** Have you ever watched a friend struggle with his need of salvation? You rejoice when he decides to accept the Lord. When you have the opportunity to lead someone to the Lord, the very first thing you do is pray for his spiritual growth. That is what Paul is doing here after spending nearly three years with them (Acts 18-21). He wants them to know how to grow in the Lord, by praying for God to give them wisdom, knowledge, and understanding (vv. 17-18). Also, that they would realize the calling they have in Christ and the power He has over the past, present, and future.

***Who have you led to the Lord lately? Pray for yourself and a friend to grow in wisdom, knowledge, and understanding of what you have in Jesus.***

Week 6

*Wednesday Ephesians 2:1-7*

Wow! What a difference Jesus makes in our lives! The first verses tell what we were before Christ (i.e. dead in sin, disobedient to God, following the world, an enemy of God, a child of wrath, and pursuing selfish desires). It was not a pretty picture. Paul tells us in the next verses what God has done for us through His grace. We become spiritually alive, elevated to a new level of life. We can have a continuous relationship with Christ! When we contrast who we were with who we are now in Christ, we can only marvel at God's great love, grace, and mercy; given freely to undeserving sinners like us.

***How has Christ changed your life? Make a list comparing how your life was before and after Christ came in. Take time to really thank Him!***

Life stEP

*Thursday Ephesians 2:8-13*

If you have been a Christian for any length of time, you've probably memorized verses 8 and 9. They may even have been instrumental in your coming to and understanding the Gospel. Look again at the three main words. *Grace* is God giving us something we don't deserve. *Faith* allows us to accept God's grace. The *gift* comes again from the hand of God. We can't boast in something we didn't earn, buy, work for, etc. When we understand all that the Lord has done for us, our response should be to do whatever He asks. His desire is for us to do good works, to do His will, to do whatever He has planned for us.

***Praise God for His grace and gift of salvation! In every choice you make today ask if it is something that will bring Him glory.***

Life stEP

Friday Ephesians 2:14-18

Q:

A:

**Digging DEEPER** There are many prejudices in our world, but praise God, He is not prejudiced! There was a huge division between Jews and Gentiles during the first century. Paul teaches that while they were once alienated, they are now one in Christ. Through Jesus, we are each reconciled first to God; then we can be reconciled with others because we share Jesus in our hearts. His desire is for us to work as one to do His good work, to not be divided, and to reach those around us with the Gospel of the Lord Jesus Christ. The bottom line is this – whether Jew or Gentile, all believers have a common denominator – new life in Christ.

**Life stEP** *Do you have Jesus as a common denominator with other believers? Take time today to thank Jesus for removing the barrier.*

Saturday Ephesians 2:19-22

Q:

A:

**Digging DEEPER** Have you ever watched a building go up? Much time is spent on getting the foundation just right, and then the rest of the building will fit together perfectly. Paul is saying we are a picture of the work of Christ in our life. We are a living temple built of people who are called *living stones* (1 Peter 2:4-8). Christ is the foundation and cornerstone. Every line in the building is justified only when it is aligned with Him. What a privilege it is to be the habitation of God! How important it is that our lives, individually and corporately demonstrate that indwelling relationship.

***Are you part of Christ's Temple with Jesus as the foundation? Welcome all believers to fellowship with you, especially those who are different from you.***

Week 7

Do you ever get tired of people telling you to just *live for Jesus* without really explaining how or why? This week Paul will reveal a mystery about Jews and Gentiles. He will offer practical advice on how and why we can live a successful Christian life in unity with others.

Prayer Focus for this week:

**Q: The QUESTION - What is the writer saying?**

**A: The APPLICATION- How can I apply this to my life?**

Sunday Ephesians 3:1-7

Q:

A:

Digging DEEPER

Why do you think Paul claimed himself to be *the prisoner of the Lord Jesus Christ* when he was in a Roman prison? He knew Whom he served and the reason he was there. It didn't matter what the Roman's did to him. He felt compelled by the Holy Spirit to explain the equality that Jew and Gentiles have in Jesus. It was a *mystery* he was sent to reveal to both, that they are one in Christ. This is the third time he addresses this issue (Ephesians 1:11-12; 2:14-18; 3:6-7). It must be something important for us to understand and remember. We are "of the same body and partakers of His promise in Christ."

***We should accept anyone into fellowship who claims the Lord Jesus Christ as his Lord and Savior. Find someone other than from your own church to fellowship with today.***

Life stEP

Monday Ephesians 3:8-13

Q:

A:

Digging Deeper

A thousand piece puzzle takes a long time and great patience to put together. Part of the problem is that some of the pieces look alike, but don't fit where you think they should. The Old Testament writers had different pieces of the puzzle. Now Paul is humbled to be given the responsibility of putting the pieces together by proclaiming the (puzzle) *mystery* of the church to the world. Because of the grace of God, Jew and Gentile are now one body in Christ. They are called the church, and through them the world is to learn of the glories of the Gospel.

***Does your piece of the puzzle fit with those around you revealing the Gospel to others? Decide to share Jesus with someone today.***

Life stEP

Tuesday Ephesians 3:14-21

Q:

A:

Digging Deeper

Have you ever been to Niagara Falls? Surely, you've seen pictures of this marvel of God's creation? Niagara Falls has just a fraction of the power that Paul is praying for *the whole family in heaven and earth.* Paul makes four requests for God's people. First, He asks they be strengthened by the Holy Spirit. Second, he asks that Christ would feel at home in their hearts. Third, he wants them to comprehend, know, and experience Christ's love. Fourth, He wants believers to understand the unlimited source we can draw from for every need.

***Pray for strength, for Christ to feel at home in your heart, to know how much Jesus loves you, and understand the unlimited source we have in the Holy Spirit. Write down one way you will live your life differently today.***

Life stEP

Week 7

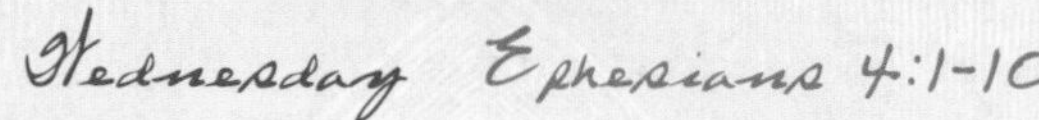


Digging DEEPER

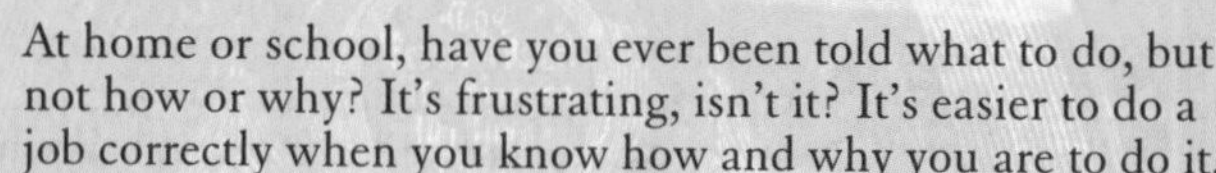

At home or school, have you ever been told what to do, but not how or why? It's frustrating, isn't it? It's easier to do a job correctly when you know how and why you are to do it. Paul followed his normal writing pattern by telling us what to do (doctrine) in the first three chapters. Now, in the next three, he will give us the how and why (practical advice). Paul tells us to walk worthy in verse 1. How? By exhibiting three qualities: lowliness (true humility), meekness (gentle control), and forbearance (patience with others). Why? As believers, we share seven *ones* in Christ. Meditate on them today.

***Are you walking worthy? Do you exhibit the three qualities? Examine the things believers have in common in Christ and walk in unity with others.***

Thursday Ephesians 4:11-16

Digging DEEPER

When was the last time you were called a *baby*? It usually means someone is saying you're behaving immaturely. That's what Paul is calling us in verse 14 if we haven't grown up spiritually. Spiritual children are often doctrinally insecure and fall when someone comes along with false teaching. It is plain in verse 14 that spiritual unity and spiritual maturity are closely linked. God gives each of us gifts and abilities to be used for His service in *the work of the ministry…and edifying the body.* We each have things we can do that others cannot. Unity in the faith needs to be our goal for God's glory and honor.

***Are you a spiritual baby? Make a list of what you can do today to mature in the faith. Use your gifts and abilities to help someone else mature.***

Life stEP

Friday Ephesians 4:17-24

Q:

A:

**Digging Deeper** Choices. We make them every day. Some may seem unimportant; however, they could make a great deal of difference to someone else. In this passage Paul gives us two choices. We either live as unbelievers or as believers living in the truth. The choice is ours. Romans 1:21-25 explains what happens to those who choose to stay in the world. Those *in Christ* will want to put off the old man, renew their mind, and put on the new man. These issues are covered more in Romans 6:6 and Colossians 3:10. The Christian life is likened to stripping off the dirty clothes of a sinful past and putting on the snowy white robes of Christ's righteousness.

*What do you need to put off and put on today?* **Life stEP**

Saturday Ephesians 4:25-32

Q:

A:

**Digging Deeper** What kind of people do you like to hang out with? Hopefully, people who will help you in your walk with the Lord and warn you when you head in the wrong direction. Paul explains four important traits to work on in our lives. We can also look for these traits in a friend: 1. Are we truthful (v. 25)? 2. How do we control anger (v. 26)? 3. Is there a problem with stealing (v. 28)? 4. What is our speech like (v. 29)? We all need to work on these traits Paul closes this chapter with some positive characteristics that should be a mark of all believers: kindness, a tender heart, and forgiveness.

***Closely examine one of these traits in your life. What can you do to improve it? Do you look for friends who will help your spiritual walk?***

Week 8

What do husbands and wives, children and parents, slaves and masters, and you and I have in common? Submission! Some people don't like to be under authority. Paul will help us understand the how's and why's of *being in Christ* and the unity we can have with others.

Prayer Focus for this week:

**Q: The QUESTION - What is the writer saying?**

**A: The APPLICATION- How can I apply this to my life?**

Sunday Ephesians 5:1-7

Q:

A:

Digging DEEPER

Did you have a dress-up box when you were little? Was there a place you could go to let your imagination run wild and pretend to be whatever you wanted to be? Paul is telling us that when we are aware of who we are doctrinally in Christ (vv. 1-3) there is to be a lifestyle worthy of that relationship. This relationship makes it possible to live a higher life than the unsaved can know – a life ordered by love. Because *God is love*, believers emulating Him will live a life that manifests that same love. If we are true followers of Christ, our desire should be to avoid the pagan pitfalls listed here and live a life pleasing to the Lord.

***Whom are you imitating or following? List two pitfalls you will put off today.***

Monday Ephesians 5:8-14

Q:

A:

**Digging Deeper** Have you ever been afraid of something (real or imagined) in the dark? Maybe it was a nightmare, strange noises, or you were in a strange place. The dark can be a scary place! In Christ we are to be lights in the world (Matthew 5:14). You should live so others will see and be drawn to the light. We are not to have fellowship with darkness, but show others where they can come to the light (John 1:9). Paul points out some contrasts between the conditions of the unbeliever and the believer. The believer has two responsibilities regarding sin. First, he must have no part in it. Second, he is to reprove such behavior in others.

***Exercise 1 John 1:9 to get rid of all sin in your own life. Now be a light of the Lord and draw someone who is in the dark to Him.***

Tuesday Ephesians 5:15-21

Q:

A:

**Digging Deeper** What does it mean to walk *circumspectly*? It means to walk *carefully* or *accurately*. We are to be wise in the choices we make everyday as to how we walk in the Lord (v. 15 and Psalm 19:7). Paul gives us some do's and don'ts. Some of the do's are: Do redeem the time (v. 16), understand what God's will is (v. 17), and be filled with the spirit (v. 18). How are we to accomplish these three huge tasks? Verses 19-21 tell us first to enjoy music with other believers and in our own heart. Then always to give thanks for everything God has done. Then we are to submit to one another.

***How are you walking? What are you doing to redeem the time? What can you do to understand God's will and be filled with the Holy Spirit?***

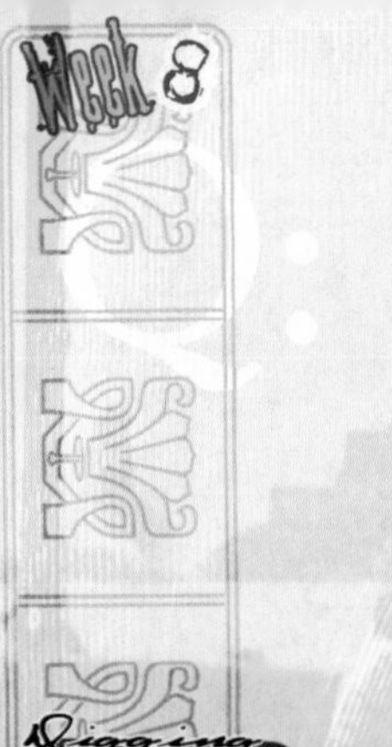

Week 8

Wednesday Ephesians 5:22-33

Digging Deeper

Are you thinking you can skip this passage? It doesn't apply to you yet. You're probably not going to get married for several years. Look again. What characteristics should you look for in a mate? Paul would suggest that you ladies look for a man who will love you as Christ does and who would be willing to die for you. Guys, you should look for a wife who will lovingly submit to your authority and reverence and respect you. When a husband practices such Christ-like love, willing submission on the part of the wife is not difficult. God intends marriage to be a picture to the world of Christ and the church.

Life Step

***Make a list of the characteristics you will look for in a mate. Follow each with a Scripture reference. What qualities do you need to develop?***

Thursday Ephesians 6:1-9

Digging Deeper

If you were raised in a Christian home, verse 1 was probably the first verse you memorized. It still applies today. Study Exodus 20:12 to see the origin of this verse and the promise it carries. From children's obedience, Paul moves to slaves' obedience. You may not think this applies to you but when you are employed, it will. You are to submit to an employer as you would the Lord Jesus. In all these basic relationships, we are to understand that no matter who we serve (spouse, parent, or employer) we are ultimately serving Christ.

Life Step

***Look again at Exodus 20:12 and examine the only promise God gave in the Ten Commandments! To whom are you submitting? Do one thing today that you know Christ wants you to do to serve Him!***

Q:

A:

Do you have all your armor in place? Step in front of God's spiritual mirror (His Word) to see what you look like. Paul explains that the battle is real and no true soldier of Jesus Christ can expect to be immune from enemy attacks. Remember he is writing from jail and fully armored soldiers are in plain view. We are to put on real (spiritual) armor so that we will be able to stand firm against a very real enemy. When examining each piece of armor Paul describes, notice there is nothing protecting the back. God expects us to face our enemy, to stand firm, and to be strong. We are always to be prepared.

*Do you have all your armor on? Which piece can you strengthen to be able to stand up to and fight a real enemy who ultimately wants to destroy you?*

Saturday Ephesians 6:18-24

Q:

A:

When we are in the middle of a battle, what is the most important weapon we have to fight the enemy? PRAYER! Our enemy makes it the most difficult weapon to use because he knows it is the most powerful. Paul tells us to pray with *prayers* and *supplications*. What's the difference? Prayer is the general term, what we're to do without ceasing (1 Thessalonians 5:17). Supplications are specific requests (Psalms 119:170). Mighty things happen when God's people pray. Read the prayers of Moses in Exodus 33:12-23, of Joshua in Joshua 10:12-15, of Solomon in 1 Kings 3:4-15, and of Hezekiah in Isaiah 37:14-38.

***Get ready to go to battle today with the knowledge of how to use the best weapon at your disposal. Read the powerful prayers listed above.***

## Week 9

**Is God really in control of everything? The book of Esther proves this truth as well as any other book in the Bible. Certain death, banished queens, lunatic kings, and a plot to hang a Jew are revealed. You have the wrong man in and the right man out. You'll have to stick with this story to the end. Don't miss a day!**

*Prayer Focus for this week:*

**Q: The QUESTION - What is the writer saying?**

**A: The APPLICATION- How can I apply this to my life?**

Sunday Esther 1:1-12

Q:

A:

**Digging DEEPER**

The story of Esther is awesome! Jews were captive in a city called Susa, and the king, Ahasuerus, also known as Xerxes, decides to throw a seven day drunken feast for all his friends. The women weren't invited, so Queen Vashti decides to throw her own party for the ladies. The drunken king wants his queen to parade around before all his drunken buddies. She refuses, and that begins an amazing story of how the Lord protected His people. Sometimes we wonder if the Lord really sees us and is working in our lives, but this book is a perfect example of God's ability to control everything and everybody. God misses nothing!

***When you know what's right, do you have the courage to stand up for it? What can you take a stand for this week? Will you?***

**Life stEP**

Monday Esther 1:13-22

Q:

A:

**Digging Deeper** All this might seem kind of ridiculous, but keep in mind the king had been drinking during this whole situation and was now very *merry with wine* (v. 10). So when he called for the queen and she refused to come and show off all her beauty, he banishes her forever. We are told to seek godly advice, but drinking and listening to bad advice of his counselors wasn't very smart. Alcohol and anger (chapter 2:1) do not make for wise decisions. But God is in control. Look at verse 19. If you compare this with Psalm 75:6-7 you'll find that it is God who *puts down one and sets up another.* The Lord is going to elevate someone to be queen that will help Israel, but the stakes are going to be high.

***Do you have problems making right decisions? Are you listening to the advice of those you can trust and will lead you in making right decisions?***

Tuesday Esther 2:1-11

Q:

A:

**Digging Deeper** Today sounds like a new reality show! It's the *Queen Hunt Makeover Show*! About four years had passed and the king's officers set out to locate the prettiest girls they could find, and the contest was on. Of all people, a young Jewish girl, Esther, was taken to the palace. Enter Mordecai and Esther. Cousin Mordecai had been like a father to Esther after her parents died. Mordecai was faithful to God and his people, and viewed Esther being in the palace as something the Lord might use for His glory. God is always in control! Sometimes we don't understand why things happen, but God can amaze you with the results!

***What difficulties have you been through recently? Can you trust God with the outcome? Have you asked God to help you learn through it?***

Wednesday Esther 2:12-23

In this passage, Esther finds favor in the sight of those over her (v. 15). We are told *that when a man's ways please the Lord He maketh even his enemies to be at peace with him* (Proverbs 16:7). The principle of 1 Samuel 2:8 – *He raiseth up…to make them inherit the throne of glory*, comes into play here as God is at work in Esther's life. He honored her actions and activities. God can still choose to use whomever He wishes to accomplish His goals and purposes. Eventually, Esther will reveal her true identity as a Jewess and win the king's favor. In the meantime, the Lord allows Mordecai to do something courageous by uncovering a plot to assassinate the king.

***List a circumstance that would allow you to identify with the Lord. Will you let your life and lip be seen and heard?***

Life stEP

Thursday Esther 3:1-15

It had been five years since Mordecai informed the king of an assassination plot. So much time had passed; his good deed had been written down but had been forgotten. Enter Haman and the development of a plan to murder the Jews. Even though Haman had gained great respect in the kingdom, when everyone but Mordecai refused to bow to him, it only fueled the fire. A date was set when all the Jews, especially Mordecai, would be destroyed. Haman's wrath was so intense that even the city was surprised and perplexed. When a person's anger is a major factor, wise decisions are rarely made. Yet God is in control. This provided the time Mordecai needed to do something about the decree.

***What causes you to get angry? When you make key decisions are you sure that you are thinking wisely… without the influence of anger?***

Life stEP

Friday Esther 4:1-17

Q:

A:

Digging DEEPER Esther lived in the palace so she was not aware of what was going on. It wasn't until she was informed of the situation with Mordecai by her maids that she learned how grave the matter really was. The solution was simple. Esther could just tell the king what was happening, right? Verse 11 is important to understand today. Even though Esther was queen, it was a somewhat dangerous position to enter the king's presence without an invitation. We know what the king did to Vashti. Killing or banishing was quite common. It did not matter who you were. The king hadn't seen Esther in a month. Should she risk it? This is her chance to show courage, but she would do nothing without getting people to fast and pray.

Life stEP *How important is prayer when it comes to making major decisions in your life? Is there something you should be praying about now?*

Saturday Esther 5:1-14

Q:

A:

Digging DEEPER Esther starts to reveal her plan. It comes in two stages or rather banquets. She could have asked the king to save her people from Haman. Instead, God uses her to inflate his ego by inviting both the king and Haman to a second banquet. Haman is obviously a very cocky guy. He boasts to everybody of this special invitation. The Lord often has a way of humbling people like that. Haman hates Mordecai intensely and plans to hang him on a 75 foot gallows, so high that everybody could see it from a distance. Mordecai will be dead before the second banquet and before Queen Esther makes her request! Time is running out… but God controls both time and circumstances, as we shall see!

*Have you left room for God to intervene in your plans? Will you submit your plans for today with Him?*

Week 10

Radical revenge and a honeymoon! That's what this week is about. We finish up Esther, and spend a couple of days in the book of Song of Solomon. It's like the latest action movie all in one week! There are good things and *bad* we learn from Esther. We also learn a couple of critical things about marriage.

Prayer Focus for this week:

**Q: The QUESTION - What is the writer saying?**

**A: The APPLICATION- How can I apply this to my life?**

Sunday Esther 6:1-14

Q:

A:

Digging DEEPER

Mordecai has one day left to live! What are the chances of the king not being able to sleep and stumbling across Mordecai's help five years earlier? Actually, with God – there are no chances. Talk about a plan that backfires! Haman selfishly thinks he's going to get the *royal treatment*, but instead the Lord honors the one person Haman hates more than anyone else. Wouldn't you have loved to have been there and seen the look on Haman's face when he discovers the king is honoring Mordecai? Talk about God in control! Just about the time Haman realizes he's got to do something, he gets whisked off to the second banquet Queen Esther has prepared. He's in for another surprise!

***Do you try to honor yourself or do you give God all the glory? Do you tend to think of others before yourself?***

Monday Esther 7:1-10

Q:

A:

Have you ever said "oops"? Today is the biggest *oops* of all time! Haman has to go to the banquet. He would be in trouble if he didn't. At the banquet Queen Esther readily identifies herself as a Jew, then carefully unveils Haman's scheme to murder her and all her people. Once this was revealed to the king, he decides to execute Haman. Nothing could conclude this story better than to hang Haman on the same gallows he intended for Mordecai. *Oops*! Nothing takes God by surprise. Centuries later people tried to destroy God's plan by crucifying Jesus, but that provided salvation for the whole world! That wasn't an *oops*; that was all in God's plan! He ***is*** in control!

***Is what you are going to do today going to find favor in God's sight? What choices do you need to make to enjoy God's blessing?***

Tuesday Esther 8:1-17

Q:

A:

Haman is not only gone, but his estate and his position are given to Mordecai. Back then, laws could not be reversed – not even by the king. Haman's decree to destroy all the Jews was still in effect. However, the king allows Mordecai to write another decree which allows the Jews the right to organize and defend themselves. There were still nine months before Haman's decree would go into effect, giving the Jews plenty of time to get ready for the attack. This message was delivered by utilizing many different people. More would be reached today if the message of the Gospel was being delivered by many more people. It's not over yet, there's still more drama to come. Stay tuned.

***Are you helping the advancement of the Gospel by sharing it with others? Who can you witness to today by testifying or handing out a Gospel tract?***

Wednesday Esther 9:1-17

Judgment day finally came. The message was so carefully proclaimed that instead of the Jews being slain and their wealth taken, it was the enemy! Some 75,000 were slain, including the ten sons of Haman, thus removing any further threat to the Jews. Interestingly enough, no plunder was taken as was permitted (8:11). God's people needed to prove that they were better than their enemies. Only when the enemy was slain did they celebrate. It is evident that God was working behind the scenes and He is very thorough.

***Have you given God thanks for any victory He has allowed you to accomplish? You can only give thanks and celebrate when the enemy is slain. What enemy in your life needs to be slain today?***

Life stEP

Thursday Esther 9:18-10:3

There are many Jews today that still celebrate the *Feast of Purim*. It came directly from this account in Esther. It is celebrated from sunset on March 24 through sunset on March 25. Another way of showing their appreciation for deliverance was by sending gifts to one another including something for those who were poor. It is always good to praise God for victories. The bottom line is this – adversaries will come and go, but nothing can happen to God's people that is not part of His plan. He is perfect and in control – always!

***What situation do you need to trust God with, and not worry? Would you pray and ask the Lord to help you, and then patiently wait for His timing?***

Life stEP

Friday Song of Solomon 2:1-17

Q:

A:

**Digging DEEPER** This is a poem about a guy and a girl falling in love. They talk about things in nature – like gardens, flowers and deer, but it's a poetic way of talking about their love for each other. The two key verses are 7 and 15. Verse 7 talks about not awakening love too soon. There are desires between guys and girls that can only be satisfied in marriage, and we should not rush love and sex. Verse 15 talks about *foxes*. The fox was an animal used to ruin crops back then. This is the young couple's way of saying they need to get rid of the things (*foxes*) in their relationship that can harm them. It's the story of their courtship and marriage.

*Are you committed to saving yourself physically and emotionally for marriage? If you've made a mistake, will you pray and re-commit yourself?* **Life stEP**

Saturday Song of Solomon 5:10-6:3

Q:

A:

**Digging DEEPER** There are a lot of things girls say about guys today, but probably nothing like this. Verses 10-16 are, loosely translated, "You're one in a million!" Chapter 5:2-6 they have a little lover's quarrel, and she wants to make up with him. He goes to a real garden, probably a place that meant something special to them both. She goes after him and they make up. In verse 3, she reaffirms her love for him. In any marriage there are challenges and quarrels, but problems have got to be solved. Lasting love takes work and a couple has to work *together* since a marriage is only stable if the husband and wife have a solid relationship. It involves romance and commitment. Divorce is not the answer; commitment to working it out is.

*Are you committed to waiting for that one person that you'll be devoted to forever? Are you in a relationship that is not honoring God?*

Week 11

What do you do if you are stuck on an island and are in a church with people who only want to cause trouble? Or what do you do with a thief who is on the run? How could you handle these problems when you're in prison yourself? That's where Paul was when he wrote the books of Titus and Philemon. Don't miss it.

Prayer Focus for this week:

**Q: The QUESTION - What is the writer saying?**

**A: The APPLICATION- How can I apply this to my life?**

Sunday Titus 1:1-9

Q:

A:

Digging DEEPER

Paul writes to a friend of his named Titus. In the past, Paul had helped Titus grow as a Christian, and now Titus was helping others grow. Titus lived on an island called Crete. There were a number of churches on that island that needed help. Paul's job was to help these churches get organized and appoint men to lead. Verses 6-9 give a list of qualities that are expected in church leaders. The key is verse nine. *Any church is just one generation away from extinction.* All you have to do is fail to pass on what God has taught you. It's the job of every person in the church to pass it on and help others grow.

***After listening to God's Word, are you committed to putting it into practice? Who can you help grow spiritually by sharing God's Word?***

Life stEP

Monday Titus 1:10-16

Q:

A:

**Digging DEEPER** The churches in Crete needed help because there were unruly and deceptive individuals in the church. Men in these churches were teaching things that were false. They were stirring up trouble because they wanted the power to do what they wanted. Were there really men like this in the church? *Yes!* It even happens today. That's why it's essential to know God's Word and practice it. Truth is either going to be taught and spread, or error will. It was Titus's job to train elders in every city. That way when error tries to creep in, they will recognize it and can deal with it. The church must follow *godly* men who follow Christ.

***Are you living an unruly life? Does your lifestyle resemble one that is in submission to the Lord? Do you willingly submit to God's Word or choose to follow your own desires?***

Tuesday Titus 2:1-10

Q:

A:

**Digging DEEPER** Paul has something to say to everybody in the church. He divided the people into five groups: older men, older women, younger women, younger men, and bondservants (workers). First, he encourages them all to speak sound doctrine – that's what the Bible says. While others teach false doctrine, it's easy to get soft or stop standing firm. Paul wanted Titus to stay strong, even though he wouldn't be very popular. Verse seven is the key. It's been said, *your talk talks, and your walk talks, but your walk talks louder than your talk talks.* Live it in front of others! Actions will always speak louder than words! We must live what we believe. If we don't live it, we really don't believe it.

***Are there any actions in your life that are not consistent with what you believe? What are you going to do to change that?***

Week 11

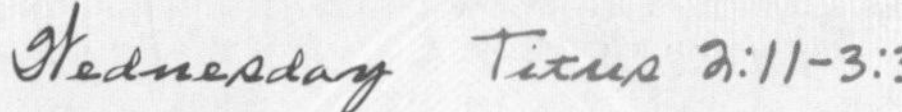

Verses 11-14 show a pattern for us to grow in Christ. God's grace came to us (people who were sinners), and He lovingly saved us (v. 11). We were unable to save ourselves. As a result of this grace we are now empowered to live a godly life. Sin should no longer master us and we should now live (v. 12) looking for His glorious appearing (v. 13). His salvation should produce a change in attitude, appetite, ambition, and action. Titus 2:1-2 share a few ways we can grow spiritually; whereas, the next verse (v. 3) describes the kind of life we had before we were saved. The emptiness is nothing we should want to go back to.

***Name two ungodly things or worldly lusts that trouble you. With God's help, will you endeavor to refuse to yield to them today? Will you demonstrate your love by changing?***

Thursday Titus 3:4-15

Paul begins by reminding them (as he did in 2:11) that their salvation is a gift from God. Their good works had nothing to do with it. His Holy Spirit had transformed (changed) them. Even their daily walk is something that He empowered by His mercy. Today this same transforming power enables us to live for Him and maintain good works. He's done it all, there is no longer any excuse for us to live like we used to. In chapter 1, Paul encourages Titus not to argue with those men that were teaching things that were false. Just stick to doing right! Don't give up! Never quit living for God. You will never regret it.

***Do you have a friend that often discourages you from living for Christ? Who would be a positive influence to help you live for God? Will you seek their help today?***

Life stEP

Friday Philemon 1-9

Q:

A:

**Digging DEEPER** Paul calls himself a prisoner "of" Jesus Christ, even though this letter was written while he was "in" a prison cell in Rome (v. 1). There is a difference. The most important reason is *who* holds him captive. Paul goes on to commend his friend, Philemon for his Christian character, but in verses 8 and 9, Paul has something serious to talk to him about. He wants Philemon to respond because of their love for each other. We'll check that out tomorrow. Romans 6:16 says we are slaves, or in this case captives, to someone. We can be slaves to our selfishness or to Christ. One way leads to life, and the other to death. The choice is yours… but not the consequences.

*Who has control over your life? List an area that you need to surrender to Christ. Will you yield it to Him today?* **Life stEP**

Saturday Philemon 10-25

Q:

A:

**Digging DEEPER** Enter Onesimus, a runaway slave, who belonged to Paul's friend, Philemon. The bad news is that not only did Onesimus run away but in the process stole something of Philemon's. It so happens, (under divine guidance) Onesimus and Paul meet and Paul has the privilege of leading him to Christ. Paul knows stealing from Philemon was wrong, and knows Onesimus must go back and make it right. Paul sends him back to Philemon with this letter offering to pay back what Onesimus stole. Paul asks Philemon for another favor… to forgive Onesimus. He is no longer an unprofitable slave, but is now a profitable brother in Christ (v. 16).

*Is there someone who has wronged you that you need to forgive? Is there one that you treat badly, that should be treated as a fellow believer?*

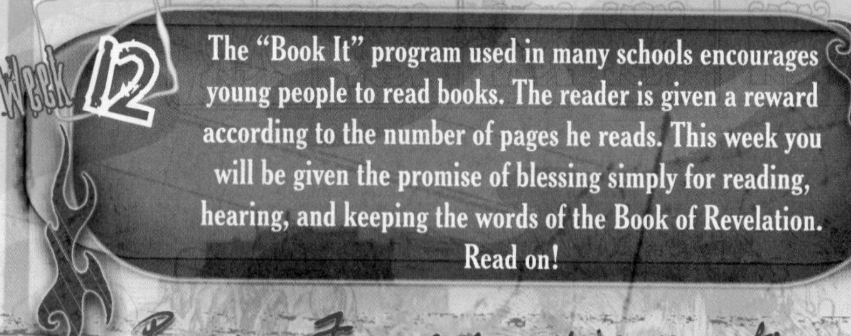

Week 12
The "Book It" program used in many schools encourages young people to read books. The reader is given a reward according to the number of pages he reads. This week you will be given the promise of blessing simply for reading, hearing, and keeping the words of the Book of Revelation. Read on!


Prayer Focus for this week:

**Q: The QUESTION - What is the writer saying?**

**A: The APPLICATION- How can I apply this to my life?**

Sunday Revelation 1:1-8

Q:

A:

Digging DEEPER

How do you feel when someone lets you in on a secret? Maybe you were kept in suspense for a long time and then, finally, they revealed their plans to you. The word *revelation* means *unveiling*. As John records the events God revealed to him, he unveiled both God's message about the future and about His Messenger – Jesus Christ. The first truth that the Apostle John unveils to the seven churches of Asia is that Jesus Christ, the One Who was, is, and is to come, would return to earth for every eye to see.

***Are you ready for His return? If Jesus Christ were to come today, are you prepared to meet Him?***

## Monday Revelation 1:9-16

Q:

A:

Have you ever seen something that "blew your mind"? Maybe it was an unbelievable stunt or an inconceivable performance. Did you ever try to describe it to a friend? While John was on the Island of Patmos, he saw and recorded a vision of the glorified Christ. After standing in awe of the Son of Man, he used the best words he could find to describe the majesty of the One whom he beheld. He compared His voice to the sound of trumpets. He compared His eyes to a burning fire, His feet to brass, His words to a sword, and His face to the brightness of the sun.

***What is your view of Jesus Christ? Is He the most awesome person you have ever met? Will you tell your friends about Him today?***

## Tuesday Revelation 1:17-20

Q:

A:

"But I just can't do it!" The task may seem overwhelming. "This is too much for me to handle." When we reach this point, it is always great when someone puts his arm around us and says, "Calm down. I'm here for you."

John faced an overwhelming experience (an experience that literally caused him to fall on his face). However, in the midst of his dramatic situation, the Lord lifted him up and let him know that everything was all right. The Lord comforted John by revealing Himself to him and giving him a task to perform.

***Will you allow the Lord to be your comfort in your next overwhelming situation? See Him for who He is and trust Him to lead you right.***

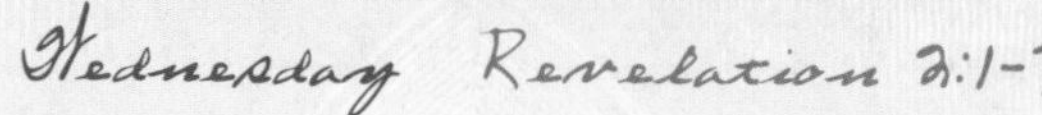

**Sunday:** Sunday school, morning service, puppet practice, evening service; **Monday:** visitation; **Tuesday:** mission service; **Wednesday:** teen group…The attitude of apathy had invaded the church at Ephesus. They were performing many good deeds and did not tolerate false teaching, but they had forgotten the reason for service. Sure, they did much to further the kingdom of God, but it was all done out of habit and ritual. They were serving the Lord because it was expected of them, not because they loved Christ.

***So, why do you do your Quiet Time? Why are you involved with Christian service projects? Is it because you ought to or is it because you want to? Spend some time right now in prayer and fall in love with Jesus Christ again.***

Life stEP

Thursday Revelation 2:8-11

Have you ever watched a news report describing the devastation of a hurricane? Year after year the meteorologists predict where hurricanes will hit. Yet as you watch the news reports, someone is bound to say something like, "This is where we live. We are not leaving. We will just rebuild and prepare for the next one." The church at Smyrna had suffered persecution and was told that more persecution was on the way. Yet, they stayed faithful to Christ despite their current persecution and the promise of more to come.

***How faithful are you to Christ? Do you stay faithful when others laugh at you for being a Christian? Will you stay faithful knowing that persecution may come in the future? Determine today that nothing will shake your faith in Christ.***

Life stEP

Friday Revelation 2:12-17

Q:

A:

**Digging DEEPER** "You scratch my back and I'll scratch yours." This was the mentality of the church at Pergamos. The Lord let them know that He was aware they lived in a difficult city. He was proud of this church that stayed faithful to His name, even to the point of death. However, He called into question their compromise. They had allowed false teaching to abide in the church. The Lord was calling them to separate themselves from the things that He hated. If they did not repent, God promised that He would judge the false teachers, and the church would be guilty by association.

**Life stEP** *From whom do you need to separate yourself? Have you allowed worldly entertainment to have a place in your life? Today is the day to repent of the sin and surrender your heart wholly to the Lord.*

Saturday Revelation 2:18-29

Q:

A:

**Digging DEEPER** A pure breed golden retriever is 100% golden retriever. In order to stay pure, the golden retriever must only mate with another golden retriever. As the fiery eyes of the Lord searched the church in Thyatira, He found a small blemish that was causing a rather large impurity. A single member of their church had been allowed to teach her false doctrine and had led many members into error. Her teachings had rendered the church impure. The Lord was going to cut out the imperfection. He encouraged the church to separate from her and to hold fast to that which is right.

***What imperfection do you need to separate yourself from in order to remain pure? Attacks from Satan are hard enough; don't allow an internal imperfection to be your downfall.***

Week 13

**Three more letters to Asian churches, John's description of Jesus Christ and the activity in His throne room, the perfect picture of worship, and the Four Horsemen of the Apocalypse are all waiting for you to discover. Read the Word of God carefully this week. His truths are fascinating.**

*Prayer Focus for this week:*

**Q: The QUESTION - What is the writer saying?**

**A: The APPLICATION- How can I apply this to my life?**

Sunday Revelation 3:1-6

Q:

A:

Digging DEEPER

For a plant to thrive, it must receive proper care. Water, the right amount of light, soil, and nutrients are necessary for growth. If a plant is deprived of any one of these requirements, it will wither and die. The church at Sardis was in the *withering* stages. The Lord told them to cultivate the little bit of life that was left in the church. He told them that if the dying church did not strengthen itself, it would ultimately die. In fact, if they did not take the appropriate steps to rejuvenate the church, the Lord would come upon it like a thief.

***How healthy is your spiritual life? Are you dying on the vine? Will you make a decision today to cultivate your Christian life with the water of the Word, the light of God's illumination, and the soil of your church? Begin to grow in Christ today.***

Life stEP

Monday Revelation 3:7-13

Q:

A:

**Digging Deeper** "I just can't do it anymore." Have these words ever run through your brain or passed through your lips? Maybe you were trying to get that last pull-up done in gym class or maybe you were refusing to give into that sin that constantly assaults you. The Lord realized that the church at Philadelphia had little strength. Nevertheless, they had clung to the Lord even when they were weak, refusing to bail out on God. He promised to keep them "from the hour of temptation." Making the decision to let go of the rope, drop off the pull-up bar, or yield to temptation may seem like the easy way to avoid a difficult situation, but in every case, you lose. Hang on! Allow God to be your strength. He will help you win.

***Will you trust Him today? Will you keep His Word so He can keep you from temptation?*** **Life stEP**

Tuesday Revelation 3:14-22

Q:

A:

**Digging Deeper** "He thinks it's all about him." "She thinks the world revolves around her." Have you ever met people like that? They are difficult to tolerate and even harder to convince of the truth. The church at Laodicea was cocky. They were sure they already had everything they needed to survive. No one could tell them anything. The Lord, however, viewed this arrogant church differently. He let them know very bluntly that they were despicable. He made it very clear that their lifestyle sickened Him so much that He wanted to vomit. Does your life nauseate God? Are you so self-absorbed that you can't hear His knock at your door?

***Will you give up your selfish ideals and open the door of your heart so Jesus Christ can come in and fellowship with you today?***

Week 13

Wednesday Revelation 4:1-11

Think of majesty. Think of splendor. Think of glorification. God brought the Apostle John into heaven and allowed him to view the future. With John's limited use of words, he begins to describe the awesomeness of the throne room of God. He describes, as best he can, four unusual creatures having six wings each. It is their continuous job to give glory and honor to God. The praise of the creatures triggers the praise of the elders and the throne room echoes in undying honor to God.

***How much do you praise the Lord? The creatures do nothing but praise Him. Today, give God the glory and honor He deserves.***

Life stEP

Thursday Revelation 5:1-7

Have you ever faced an impossible task? When you get into a situation where no one can help you, life can get a little frustrating. John described a situation that was so frustrating that it brought tears to his eyes. No one was worthy to open the book God held in His hand. As John wept over the situation, one of the elders revealed that the Lion of the tribe of Judah was worthy to open the book. However, when John turned around to see this "Lion," he saw a Lamb who looked as if He had been slain. John saw the only worthy One, Jesus Christ, take the book from the hand of God.

***How do you see Jesus Christ? He is the Lion of the tribe of Judah and the Lamb of God who takes away the sin of the world. Will you worship the Lamb because He is King?***

Life stEP

Friday Revelation 5:8-14

Q:

A:

Digging DEEPER What is your definition of worship? The Apostle John describes sincere worship of Jesus Christ in this chapter. Worship is *giving something its worth.* The elders, who were the redeemed, (and thus human), sang praises to Jesus Christ simply because He was worthy to open the book. Notice, however, that their worship was not limited to singing (vv. 12-13). They, in unison, said that Jesus Christ was worthy "to receive power and riches, and wisdom and strength and honor and glory and blessing." The Lamb that was slain is alive forevermore and is worthy to receive endless praise.

***How much do you praise the Lord? Without singing or worship songs, how will you worship Jesus Christ? Will you commit to worshipping Him more genuinely today?*** Life stEP

Saturday Revelation 6:1-8

Q:

A:

Digging DEEPER In the 1990's, the Four Horsemen of the World Wrestling Federation (WWF) were a symbol of the fact that other wrestlers would be feeling sure pain. Those four, however, never inflicted as much pain and sorrow on the human race as the original Four Horsemen of the Apocalypse will. The rider of the white horse carries a bow without arrows and represents conquest through a political takeover. The red horse is a symbol of war and will steal peace from the earth. With the arrival of the black horse comes famine. The inflated price of wheat and barley reveal the high level of demand and the low level of supply. The pale horse brings death. Those who have not accepted Christ will face these coming judgments.

***Are you prepared to meet Christ? Which of your friends will you warn of these future events?***

Week 04

No Hollywood horror film can compare to the description of destruction, terror, and chaos found in the pages of Revelation. The evil creatures from the bottomless pit are unleashed on the earth, but some people will be protected from this bedlam. Find out who is spared as you read these chapters from the Word of God this week.

Prayer Focus for this week:

**Q: The QUESTION - What is the writer saying?**

**A: The APPLICATION- How can I apply this to my life?**

Sunday Revelation 6:9-17

Q:

A:

Digging DEEPER

If you have ever wondered what the tribulation period will be like, John gives a vivid description. Jesus Christ opens the fifth seal and John views the souls of countless martyrs longing for some type of vindication. When they were given white robes, they were told to rest until other martyrs had fulfilled their calling. When the sixth seal was opened, the natural structure of the universe is jolted out of alignment. The earth suffers a great earthquake. The sun refuses to give her light. The moon appears as blood. The stars fall to the earth with catastrophic effects. The mighty men of the earth will seek death as an alternative to the wrath of Jesus Christ.

*Jesus Christ possesses limitless power. How can you give Him the proper respect today?*

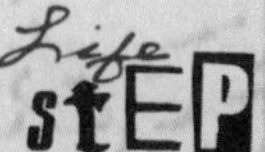

Monday Revelation 7:1-8

Q:

A:

**Digging DEEPER** Let's take a break! It's as if the writer of Revelation is given time off from death and destruction. Between the sixth and seventh seal, John gives his readers a breath of fresh air. He reports that 144,000 men (Revelation 14:4) are sealed with a mark. Once they are marked, God Himself protects them. The Bible is very clear that these 144,000 are all of Hebrew descent. They are preserved for the purpose of evangelism. Some groups teach that only these 144,000 will go to heaven. Others teach that anyone who accepts Christ after the Rapture will be part of this 144,000. According to the Bible, these Hebrew witnesses will win others to Christ during the tribulation period. God will protect His children.

**Life stEP** ***How has God protected you this week? Are you His child and worthy of His protection?***

Tuesday Revelation 7:9-17

Q:

A:

**Digging DEEPER** Do you ever desire to do great things for God? Have you ever wished that your life could impact many for Christ? Because of the sealing of the witnesses (vv. 7:1-8), John sees an innumerable host of people standing before the throne of God. In verse 14, we are told that they are people who have come out of the Great Tribulation as children of God. Because the 144,000 witnesses did their job, many people in the tribulation period will come to know Christ. Wow! What an impact! You can make an impact as well. The 144,000 witnesses simply fulfilled the task that God had purposed them to do. If God has saved you, your task is to be a witness for Him before the Rapture.

***How many people will come to Christ because of your willingness to fulfill your task? How will you be a witness for Christ?***

Wednesday Revelation 8:1-13

Before a tornado hits, the wind may die down and the air may become very still. This is what is known as "the calm before the storm." As the final seal is opened, an eerie silence covers the heavens. After thirty minutes of tranquility, seven angels prepare to sound their trumpets. The first angel uses hail and fire to destroy one-third of all vegetation on the earth. The second angel turns one-third of the oceans into blood. This causes the death of one-third of the sea creatures and the destruction of one-third of the ships. The third angel attacks the fresh water with poison. The fourth angel attacks the heavenly lights, but the worst is yet to come.

***If you knew that a great tornado was coming, would you not warn others to seek protection? Will you tell others of their only protection from the Great Tribulation?***

Thursday Revelation 9:1-12

After reading Revelation 9:1-12, one might feel as though he had seen a horror film. When the bottomless pit is unlocked, a swarm of evil creatures comes out of the pit. These hideous locusts are described as having the face of a man but the body of a horse. They had long hair like a woman and teeth like a lion. They could fly and when they did, it sounded like an army of chariots going into battle. The worst part of these creatures was the sting of their tail. John reported that if these locusts stung a man, the pain would be with him for five months and he would be unable to die. The name of their king, Abaddon, means *destroyer*. What a true description of their task!

***Will you fear God now with reverential awe? Or will you fear God later in sheer terror?***

# Friday Revelation 9:13-21

Q:

A:

**Digging Deeper** As if the locust creatures of Revelation 9:1-2 were not enough, the sixth angel sounds his trumpet and ushers in tribulation woe number two. An army of 200 million is unleashed on the earth with one purpose in mind – to kill one-third of all men. The "horses" that they travel on are dragon-like creatures. They have heads like a lion but can breathe out fire and brimstone. They have tails like a snake, but each tail has a head that can cause pain as well. These creatures will kill one-third of all mankind, but like Pharaoh of Egypt, the remaining two-thirds of mankind will refuse to repent of their wickedness.

**Life stEP** *Has God been trying to get your attention? Is there a sin that you need to surrender? What will God have to do to get your attention?*

# Saturday Revelation 10:1-11

Q:

A:

**Digging Deeper** Six of the seven angels have sounded their trumpets. Tribulation woe number three is yet to take place. An angel who is holding a little scroll descends from heaven. As his thunderous voice is heard, John begins to write down the actions of each thunder. Before he can write, he is told not to write about the thunders. Obviously, there is more to the Tribulation than man is privileged to know. After the angel speaks, John is told to "eat up" (read and internalize) the book that the angel has. It is sweet to the taste because it is the Word of God, yet it is bitter because it is a judgment upon the earth. John would have to prophesy the words of this book to the world.

**Life stEP** *How strong is your faith in God? When you don't have all the answers, will you still trust in Him?*

Week 15

God sends two witnesses to Jerusalem to proclaim His name, a giant earthquake rocks the city, and the Tribulation is visited in an overview form all in this week's Quiet Time. Failing to read this week's Scripture would leave a giant gap in your knowledge of the future.

Prayer Focus for this week:

**Q: The QUESTION - What is the writer saying?**

**A: The APPLICATION- How can I apply this to my life?**

Sunday Revelation 11:1-12

Q:

A:

Digging DEEPER

Do people hate you because you are a Christian? John records the actions of two witnesses that God sends to earth. During their 1,260 days of prophecy, God gives them the power to breathe fire from their mouth to destroy any would-be attackers. Because they perform similar miracles to those of Elijah and Moses, it is possible that they are these two Old Testament saints. When the 1,260 days of prophecy are past, the Lord will allow them to be killed. During the three days that they are dead, the people of earth will send gifts to one another with rejoicing over the death of these witnesses. They refuse to bury their bodies because they hate them so much. After three days, they come back to life.

*Why does the world hate Christians so much? How will you love your enemy today?*

Monday Revelation 11:13-19

Q:

A:

Digging Deeper

Have you ever experienced an earthquake? Maybe you have seen the devastation of one. As the second woe ends and the two witnesses ascend back into heaven, a great earthquake rocks the city of Jerusalem killing seven thousand men and causing even unbelievers to glorify God. As the seventh angel sounds his trumpet, the triumph of Christ is announced and the twenty-four elders worship God. As the heavens open and the ark is revealed, the earth experiences lightning, thunder, voices, an earthquake, and great hail All reveal the power of God Almighty. An earthquake should remind us that God is more powerful than we are. The 24 elders remind us to worship Him.

*How will you worship Christ today? Will you praise Him for His power?*

Life stEP

Tuesday Revelation 12:1-9

Q:

A:

Digging Deeper

"And she brought forth her firstborn Son and wrapped Him in swaddling clothes and laid Him in a manger…" (Luke 2). Revelation gives a different view of the birth of Christ. The woman represents Israel. The twelve stars are the twelve tribes of Israel. The child is Jesus Christ. The great red dragon is a picture of Satan who has a desire to destroy Jesus. Verse 4 records the fact that Satan took one-third of the angels (stars) with him when he was cast from heaven. From the time of Christ's birth, Satan has desired to destroy Him, but God has a master plan and He is in control.

*Do you trust the Lord even when His ways are confusing? How will you show Him that you trust Him today? List the ways that God has been faithful to you, then thank Him for His faithfulness.*

Life stEP

## Wednesday Revelation 12:10-17

When someone accuses you of doing wrong, how do you react? Satan spends his time in the throne room of God making accusations against Christians. After a war with Michael the archangel, Satan is kicked out of heaven and confined to the earth. Because he is confined to earth, he begins to persecute the "seed of the woman." However, God protects His children by providing a place of refuge in the wilderness for a time (1 year) and times (2 years) and half a time (1/2 years). When Satan realizes that Israel is protected, in his anger he prepares to go to war with her. The Lord is the Savior. Satan is the accuser.

***Will you live in victory because of His salvation or in defeat because of Satan's accusations? What will you do today to defy Satan?***

## Thursday Revelation 13:1-10

How do you feel when you find out something is phony? If someone pretends to be one thing and turns out to be something different, does that frustrate you? Satan (the dragon) will give power to the Beast (Antichrist) to "resurrect" from the dead, to rule for 3½ years and to be worshipped by many. During his rule, he will openly speak out against Jesus Christ. He will make war with the saints and defeat them. Any unsaved person at this time will worship the Antichrist. Satan is a phony. He tries to imitate Jesus' actions while He was on the earth. When we ally ourselves with Satan, we choose to be friends with a fake.

***This week, how can you cast off the phony works of the devil? Will you join teams with a "phony christ" or with the Real One?***

Life stEP

Q:

A:

Digging DEEPER The Godhead is made up of three persons – the Father (God), the Son (Jesus Christ), and the Spirit (the Holy Spirit). Satan, the phony, will try to mimic this unique union – the dragon (Satan) as "the father;" (the Beast) the Antichrist, as "the son," and the second Beast (the False Prophet) "the spirit." This false prophet will direct worship to the Antichrist. With his deceptive miracles, he will persuade many to worship the Beast. Those that refuse will be killed. He will connect the economic structure of the earth with loyalty to the Antichrist. Anyone who does not receive the mark of the Beast ("666") will not be able to buy or sell.

*How can you be sure you do not fall for Satan's counterfeits? Will you make a commitment today to study that which is true so you will not fall for a fake?* Life stEP

Saturday Revelation 14:1-7

Q:

A:

Digging DEEPER If you were drowning in a pool, and someone rescued you, what would your opinion of him be? Would you have a high respect for him? Would you tell others of his actions? In chapter 14 (the Tribulation in review), Jesus Christ appears on the Temple Mount with the 144,000 witnesses who have been redeemed. These witnesses are probably virgin males who are strongly tied to Christ or at least faithfully married men who have not been defiled by immorality (Hebrews 13:4). After this appearance of Christ, an angel, having the "everlasting salvation," instructs the inhabitants of the earth to fear, glorify, and worship God.

*Have you received God's salvation? Have you been rescued from the cesspool of sin? If you have, how will you fear, glorify, and worship God today?*

Week 13

**The sight of things that are unbelievable is just a few pages ahead in Scripture. The final seven vial judgments are poured out on the earth in a "grand finale" style. The blood of millions of soldiers will flow four feet deep in a valley 200 miles in length. An evil woman, a weird beast, and Christ claim the victory.**

*Prayer Focus for this week:*

**Q: The QUESTION - What is the writer saying?**

**A: The APPLICATION- How can I apply this to my life?**

*Sunday Revelation 14:8-13*

Q:

A:

**Digging DEEPER**

Would you join a team if you knew for sure that the team would lose? If defeat were guaranteed, how anxious would you be to get involved? The Bible records the fact that the Antichrist and his government (Babylon) will be defeated. During the tribulation, anyone who joins the Antichrist by receiving his mark will get severe, undiluted judgment. On the other hand, an angel announces that the children of God who die in the Tribulation are blessed. It will be better for them to die than to finish out the rest of the Tribulation. By doing the works of Satan today you are joining his team. He will ultimately be defeated.

***What will you do today to show that you are on God's team?***

Monday Revelation 14:14-20

Q:

A:

**Digging DEEPER** Have you ever been grounded or had the keys to the car taken away because of disobedience? At the time, it probably felt like the worst thing in the world. Your parents have the right and authority to punish your improper behavior, but John records the punishment of those who disobey God. The "reaping" in this passage is referring to judgment. The nations who rise up against God will be destroyed. A winepress is used to crush grapes to make grape juice. When God crushes these nations, their blood will flow over four feet deep for 200 miles. The punishment that God delivers will be swift and just.

*If you are a born again believer, will you spend some time right now thanking God for sparing you from His wrath?*

**Life stEP**

Tuesday Revelation 15:1-8

Q:

A:

**Digging DEEPER** Have you ever watched a television show that ended with the words "To be continued"? All week you waited in anticipation to see what would happen? After reading Revelation 10, it seems like there was a break in the action. In chapters 11-14, John took a break from recording judgments and turned to speak the prophecy of the "little book" that he "ate up" in chapter 10. In chapter 15, he finally allows the judgments "to be continued." After the Tribulation saints sing a worship song to Christ, seven angels are given a vial (bowl) judgment, which they will pour out on the earth.

*Knowing that God will one day judge His enemies, whom will you warn? Instead of being frustrated with the arrogance of sinful man, will you trust that one day God will settle the score?*

**Life stEP**

Week 16

## Wednesday Revelation 16:1-12

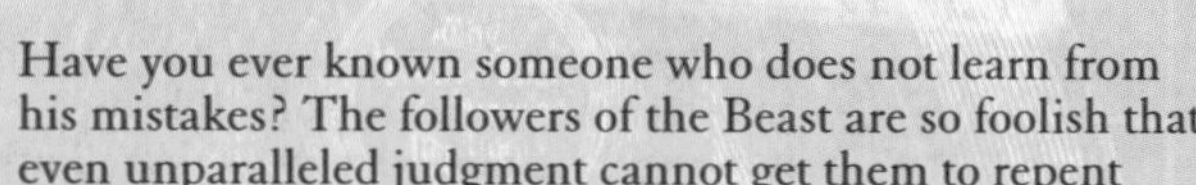

Digging Deeper

Have you ever known someone who does not learn from his mistakes? The followers of the Beast are so foolish that even unparalleled judgment cannot get them to repent from their sinful ways. They become the recipient of great sores. The entire sea clots up, like the blood of a dead man, killing all sea creatures. The third angel turns the fresh water into blood. The fourth angel uses the sun to burn men and scorch them with a great heat. The fifth angel causes darkness to cover the earth and the sixth angel dries up the great Euphrates River. Through all this the followers of the Beast "repented not of their deeds" (v. 11).

Life stEP

***How far does God have to go to get your attention? Will you commit to repenting of your sin quickly so God does not have to discipline you?***

## Thursday Revelation 16:13-21

Digging Deeper

Anyone who has ever watched a fireworks' display knows that the best part is the end. The *grand finale* is the climax of an unforgettable display of power. Much like fireworks, the seventh vial judgment ends with a gigantic "bang." The great sores, the water turning to blood, the scorching sun, the darkness and the dried up river were just the beginning. Using a giant earthquake, God caps off His powerful display. The earthquake destroys every city, flattens every mountain, and wipes out every island. To top off the earthquake, 100-pound hailstones fall, destroying more life on earth. In the midst of all the terror, anyone who watches for the return of Christ is blessed (v. 15).

Life stEP

***Do you anticipate Christ's return? What can you do today to be ready?***

## Friday Revelation 17:1-8

Q:

A:

**Digging DEEPER** Did you ever see something that totally amazed you? *Ripley's Believe It or Not* is famous for bizarre scenes. After the seven vial judgments, John is taken into the wilderness by an angel so he can view an unbelievable judgment. When John first sees the Beast and the woman, he is stunned. The royally dressed woman is partnered with all types of evil. She represents Babylon, the government system of the Antichrist. She is responsible for the death of many saints. The Beast that she rides "was, and is not, and yet is." In other words, he was alive, he died, but he came back to life. Satan is deceptive. You must know the real thing so you do not fall for his powerful trick.

**Life stEP** *Will you commit today to study God's Word for five more minutes each day so you can know the truth better?*

## Saturday Revelation 17:9-18

Q:

A:

**Digging DEEPER** It is easy when reading this passage to scratch your head and say, "I don't get it. It's too confusing." This passage contains a lot of imagery. The seven heads are really mountains and have kings. Each king represents a great world leader. The ten horns are ten kings that ally themselves with the beast in an attempt to conquer the "Lamb" of God. It is shown here by the many "waters" that the people groups of the earth will follow the beast. Despite the imagery, verse 14 presents the climax of the matter. This beast, with the people and the kings of the earth, try to make war with the Lamb of God and they fail miserably. Even the most powerful ruler on earth will one day kneel before Jehovah Sabbaoth.

**Life stEP** *How can you worship the King of kings today?*

Week 17

Satan's destruction is in sight. The city of Babylon will fall this week. The birds of the earth will eat the carcasses of dead soldiers. The wedding of Jesus Christ and His bride takes place and Satan is bound for 1,000 years. Whether you are a guy or a girl, this week's Quiet Time has something for you. Don't miss out!

Prayer Focus for this week:

**Q: The QUESTION - What is the writer saying?**

**A: The APPLICATION- How can I apply this to my life?**

Sunday Revelation 18:1-8

Q:

A:

Digging DEEPER

Have you ever met someone who thought he was *untouchable*? Maybe it was the principal's son at your school. His dad is in charge so he thinks he can break the rules and be fine. The great city of Babylon thought she was above the rules. She was wicked and filthy (v. 2). She caused others to be wicked as well (v. 3). She had gotten God's attention by the magnitude of her sin (v. 5). She thought she would never be judged (v. 7). The truth is she was going to reap twice as much evil as she sowed (v. 8). God tells His people to separate from her or they would receive judgment as well.

***Knowing that all sin will be judged, what evil practice or habit will you separate from today? Will you commit right now to do it?***

Life stEP

Monday Revelation 18:9-19

Q:

A:

Digging Deeper "It all depends on whom you trust." The kings of the earth, who had trusted their *security* to Babylon, cried because Babylon had fallen. The merchants of the earth, who had trusted their *wealth* to Babylon, cried because she had fallen. The shipmasters and sailors, who had trusted their *occupation* to Babylon, cried because she had fallen. It is interesting to note that the kings (v. 10), the merchants (v. 15), and the shipmasters (v. 17) all "stood afar off." They allowed their beloved city, once she was destroyed, to go down by herself. They used her for their gain in good times but "stood afar off" when she burned. Satan can bring you prosperity, but it will be temporary.

***Will you decide today to trust in God alone? What can you do today to prove your loyalty to Jesus Christ?*** Life stEP

Tuesday Revelation 18:20-24

Q:

A:

Digging Deeper All of your life you have probably been taught to be a good sport. When you won a game in little league, you probably had to shake hands with the other team. That mentality is tremendous and proper to have in sporting events; however, when Satan's team loses it should be reason for God's people to celebrate! Christians are told to rejoice because Babylon had fallen (v. 20). When she received her just reward, it should be the cause of much rejoicing. No longer would jubilation be in her streets. She had shed the blood of prophets and saints and no longer would she be allowed to continue. Praise the Lord!

***How will you act today in a way that will make Satan lose? What action will you take today that will damage Satan's attempts to control you?*** Life stEP

## Wednesday Revelation 19:1-8

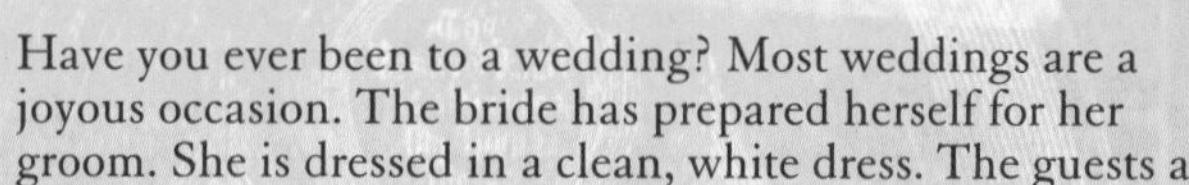

Digging Deeper

Have you ever been to a wedding? Most weddings are a joyous occasion. The bride has prepared herself for her groom. She is dressed in a clean, white dress. The guests at the wedding are joyful and singing the praises of the couple. In Revelation 19, we see the "Marriage of the Lamb." The bride of Christ had been given white clothes. No longer was she impure. She has prepared herself for her marriage to the Lamb. What a joyous occasion! The church is united with her Savior. Will you be part of this blessed arrangement? Only those who have accepted Christ will be part of the bride of Christ.

Life Step

***Who will you tell today about this future ceremony? Who can you talk to today about accepting Christ?***

## Thursday Revelation 19:9-16

Digging Deeper

Have you ever been to a gathering when the President of the United States spoke? When the announcement, "Ladies and gentlemen: The President of the United States," is spoken, the crowd claps and cheers as the Commander-in-Chief enters the room. When the Lord comes back, the fanfare will dwarf the celebration of any world leader. Jesus will ride in on a white horse to judge and make war. His clothes will remind all of the blood that He shed for them. The armies of heaven will follow Him as He smites the nations with the Word of His mouth and begins to rule with an iron rod. He has this right because He is the King of kings and Lord of lords.

***How much respect do you have for political leaders? How much more respect should you have for Jesus Christ?***

Life Step

Friday Revelation 19:17-21

Q:

A:

When an animal dies in the wild it does not take long for some type of vulture to find the carcass and begin to feast. As the King of kings and Lord of lords arrives on the scene, an angel invites all the birds of the heavens to gather for a feast. Immediately, the Lord captures both the beast and the false prophet and casts them alive into a lake of fire. The armies that remain without their leader are killed by a few simple words from the Word of God. Every bird on the planet fills his belly with the flesh of the dead. What a gruesome scene! Satan's armies are destroyed by the words of God. God has left His Word, the Bible, for us to meditate on.

***Will you have enough respect for God's Word that you will read it daily? Will you begin today?***

Life stEP

Saturday Revelation 20:1-6

Q:

A:

Digging DEEPER

"Okay, everyone, take five." Such a phrase is common in show business. The actors are given a short five-minute break. Here in Revelation, it is as if God says, "Okay, everyone, take 1,000" (years, that is). Since the first sin of Adam, the world had yet to have a break from the terrible reign of Satan. Finally, it comes. Satan is bound in the bottomless pit for 1,000 years. During this time Christians will reign with Christ on earth. The second death has no power over those who reign with Christ in the millennium. However, Satan will be allowed out of the pit for a short period of time (v. 3).

***Which event will you be part of: the first resurrection or the second death? Be sure today that the second death is not an option for you!***

Week 18

This week we will see Satan get his final shot to overthrow Jesus Christ. The old serpent will be cast into the lake of fire forever and ever. You will get a personal tour of your new home where God will rule and reign with His children. If you read the back of this book, you will see that He wins!

Prayer Focus for this week:

**Q: The QUESTION - What is the writer saying?**

**A: The APPLICATION- How can I apply this to my life?**

Sunday Revelation 20:7-15

Q:

A:

Digging DEEPER

"Ok, I'll give you one more try." Have you ever said this to someone? Maybe you have been arm-wrestling your little brother and he still thinks he can win. You know what the outcome will be, but to humor him, you give him one more shot. For reasons unknown to us, God allows Satan out of the pit long enough for him to gather an army to attempt an overthrow of Christ. This time God simply causes the recruits to go down in flames. Finally, the devil will be cast into the lake of fire and tormented forever. All the unsaved, both small and great, will be judged at the Great White Throne resulting in the second death.

***Are you on the winning side? Who will you talk to about joining the winning side today?***

Life stEP

Monday Revelation 21:1-8

Q:

A:

**Digging DEEPER** "In the beginning God created the heavens and the earth" (Genesis 1:1), "And I saw a new heaven and a new earth" (Revelation 21:1). A lot has happened between the first chapter of Genesis and the last chapter of Revelation. Now after the millennium (1007 years), John sees the New Jerusalem come down out of heaven. God decides that He is going to be with His people. In the New Jerusalem there will be no tears, no death, no sorrow, no crying, no pain, and everything will be new. One the other hand, the second death will be home to the fearful, the unbelieving, abominable, murders, whoremongers, liars, etc. Quite a contrast!

***Those who follow God will inherit life with Him. Those who follow Satan will inherit death with him. What will you inherit at the end of time?***

Tuesday Revelation 21:9-16

Q:

A:

**Digging DEEPER** "What did it look like?" Has anyone ever asked you to describe something to them? John has the awesome task of describing the New Jerusalem to all men both in his time and in the future. The first thing that John reports about the New Jerusalem is that it contains the glory of God (v. 11). The light of the city is as bright as a pure jasper stone. A great wall with twelve gates surrounds the city. Each side has three gates and at each gate stands an angel. Above the top of each gate is written one of the names of the twelve tribes of Israel. As John measures the city, each side is the same length as the other. It is 1500 miles on each side.

***Can you imagine what God has in store for His children? If He tells us this much, imagine how much is beyond our comprehension?***

Wednesday Revelation 21:17-27

Take a walk through a good jewelry store and the beauty of the jewels will amaze you. Find the most beautiful emerald. Now imagine that it is 1500 miles long and 1500 miles wide. Fifteen hundred miles is the size of the foundation of the New Jerusalem. Then multiply that one foundation by twelve because the city has twelve foundations. What a sight the city must be! Can you imagine one pearl that would fit a gate for a wall that is 216 feet high? All these precious gems are not the best part of the New Jerusalem. The best part is God's presence is there! This New Jerusalem has a temple (v. 22), light (v. 23), and safety (v. 25). Without things that defile and things that are abominable, it will be the perfect place to live.

***Will you thank the Lord for His future blessing? Will you live today in light of your future home?***

Thursday Revelation 22:1-7

"So, how does it end?" Jesus Himself reminds the readers of Revelation about the promise of this book. The person who keeps the prophecy of this book is blessed. He begins our blessing prematurely by giving us a preview of heaven. A river will proceed from God's throne. The Tree of Life will once again be available to man. It has the unique ability to bear twelve different fruits. The curse of the Garden of Eden will be lifted. He reminds us one more time that heaven will have no darkness, but most importantly God will reign forever and ever (v. 5).

***Now that you know the rest of the story, how will you live in light of this knowledge? Does knowing that God will reign forever change your perspective on God? How?***

Life stEP

Friday Revelation 22:8-15

Q:

A:

Digging DEEPER Many times e-mail messages will pop onto your screen with the request to forward it to all your friends. Here in Revelation, John was told by God to make sure he was not the one who broke the "chain letter." The letter of Revelation is about finished. Are you going to talk about it or shut the prophecy up? God told John not to shut up the prophecy because it could happen at any moment. The same is true today. The words of this prophecy need to be proclaimed to the whole earth. It is all about Jesus. When John tries to worship the angel, he is told to get off his face and worship God alone. Jesus is the Alpha and Omega and He will reward every man according to his works.

*How will you be rewarded? Will you "shut-up" the words of this prophecy or will you help keep it going?* Life stEP

Saturday Revelation 22:16-21

Q:

A:

Digging DEEPER "It's perfect." Okay, so nothing in this world is perfect, right? Wrong! John gives two warnings to all mankind. The first is, "If any man shall add unto these things, God will add unto him the plagues…" The second is, "If any man shall take away from the words of the book of this prophecy, God shall take away his part out of the book of life." Since this is the final book of the Bible, these statements can be made not only of this book, but also of the entire Bible. If you cannot add to it to make it better and you cannot take away something to make it better, then it is perfect. Even though we have the perfect Word of God, God desires to dwell with us. So, He promises to return. To which our only response should be, "Even so, come, Lord Jesus."

*Are you living in light of His return? Do you anticipate seeing Jesus Christ?*

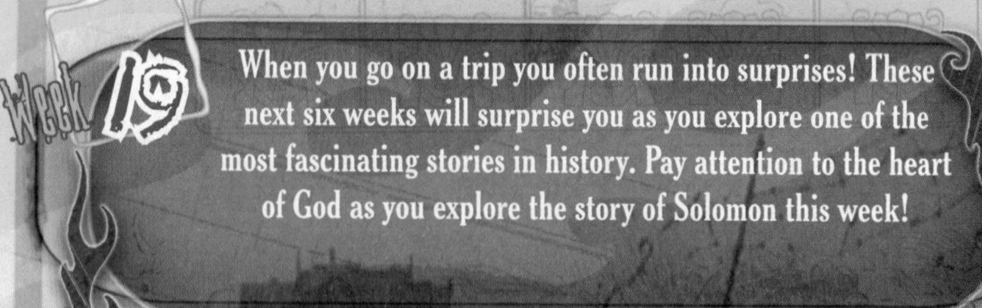

Week 19
When you go on a trip you often run into surprises! These next six weeks will surprise you as you explore one of the most fascinating stories in history. Pay attention to the heart of God as you explore the story of Solomon this week!


Prayer Focus for this week:

**Q: The QUESTION - What is the writer saying?**

**A: The APPLICATION- How can I apply this to my life?**

Sunday 1 Kings 1:15-18, 29-37

Q:

A:

**Digging DEEPER**

1 Kings, chapter one, tells the intriguing story of Adonijah, one of David's sons, declaring himself king. Adonijah was the brother of Absalom who had died eight years earlier trying to be king himself (2 Samuel 18:15). Unfortunately, David had not taught his son, Adonijah, discipline or self-control (v. 5-6). Solomon, David's son by Bath-sheba, was the son that had been chosen by God to be king (1 Chronicles 22:9), and this is exactly what happens as we finish chapter 1. God had a work for Solomon to do and God worked out that will, in spite of the desires of sinful men.

***Can you see God working in the circumstances of your family life, even though things may not be perfect at home? What is God teaching you about His will through your family?***

**Life stEP**

Monday 1 Kings 2:1-12

Q:

A:

**Digging DEEPER** King David is giving his final advice to his son, King Solomon. He instructs Solomon to be a man of courage by obeying the Word of God as written in the Law of Moses (Genesis through Deuteronomy). This will be the only way to truly prosper. God will keep His promise to Solomon (v. 4), a promise that He gave to David in the Davidic Covenant (2 Samuel 7:12-13). Now Solomon would have to act on what he had been instructed to do by carrying out capital punishment on David's enemies. While it is never our place to seek revenge, this was Solomon's proper role as king, but would be something hard for him to do.

*Are you living a life of courage by living in obedience to the Word of God? Are you walking in His ways and keeping His statutes? Are you doing all God's Word is teaching you to do today?*

**Life stEP**

Tuesday 1 Kings 3:1-15

Q:

A:

**Digging DEEPER** How do you see yourself? Solomon saw himself as a little child. God gave him a chance to ask for anything he wanted and he asked for "understanding to discern judgment" (v. 11). Solomon "loved the Lord" (v. 3), he respected his father, David (vv. 6-7), and he cared for other people instead of only himself (v. 9). No wonder God was impressed by his humble spirit. He gave him more than he asked for. God granted him not only a wise and understanding heart, but also riches and honor (v. 13).

*What are you asking God for today? Are you praying for an understanding heart? Do you love the Lord like Solomon?*

**Life stEP**

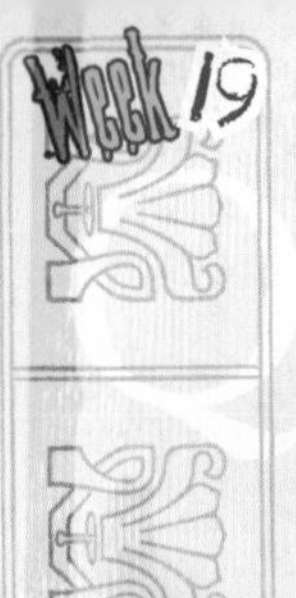

Wednesday 1 Kings 3:16-28

Digging DEEPER

Have you ever been asked a really hard question or been forced to make a really tough decision? Maybe you have been called upon to settle an argument between two friends. Maybe you have to make a decision between parents who do not agree. Solomon had asked God for understanding and God granted him a wise and understanding heart. Now, he must make a decision in an argument between two prostitutes about a living child. The stakes are high, but God gives Solomon the wisdom to give the right answer. The child is given to the real mother and the truth is made known.

***What hard decision do you have to make today? Are you praying for wisdom? God will give you wisdom just like He gave Solomon if you will just ask Him for it (James 1:5).***

Life stEP

Thursday 1 Kings 4:20-34

God answered Solomon's prayer and gave him more than he asked or even imagined (1 Kings 3:12-13). When you read the list of all the *things* that God gave Solomon (vv. 22-28), it is staggering. When you read about the wisdom that God gave him (vv. 29-34), it is truly amazing. God gave him wisdom and enlarged his heart to be interested in knowledge and to care for people. Look at all the subjects he mastered in verses 32-33. Everybody wanted to come and learn from Solomon. This is what God can do for a person who loves the Lord (1 Kings 3:3) and asks for understanding to lead God's people (1 Kings 3:9).

***What are you asking God for? Be sure to ask God for wisdom today. Who knows what other blessings He will give you as you seek to honor Him with your life (1 Kings 3:12-13).***

Life stEP

Friday 1 Kings 6:1-14, 38

Q:

A:

Digging DEEPER

Finally, Solomon's temple is built as described in chapter 6. There are several "temples" in Scripture. First, there is the tabernacle of Moses mentioned in Hebrews. Second, there is Solomon's temple here. Third, there is a smaller temple built by the returning exiles from Babylon. Last, there is the ornate Herod's temple (the one in Jesus' day). The greatest temple will be built during the millennial reign of Christ. The body of every believer in Jesus Christ is also a temple of the Holy Spirit (1 Corinthians 6:11). As beautiful as Solomon's temple was, it would only have God's blessing on it as long as they were obedient.

Life stEP

***How are you treating your body, the temple of the Holy Spirit? Only obedience to God's Word will bring God's blessing. Are you obeying God's Word in every part of your life today?***

Saturday 1 Kings 11:1-13

Q:

A:

Digging DEEPER

It's finally finished! The temple is complete. But now, something terrible happens. Solomon, a king blessed by the Lord with wisdom and treasure, a man who walked so closely with God, fell into sin. The fellowship he enjoyed with God was broken. He disobeyed God's commandment by taking more than one wife (Deuteronomy 17:16-17), and he married women who worshipped false gods. Solomon's sin was gradual. It happened over time with one sinful decision after another.

Life stEP

***God has promised that we do not have to fall into Satan's temptation like Solomon did (1 Corinthians 10:12-13). Are there any areas in your life that you have disobeyed the clear teaching of Scripture? Is there anything in your life today that you love more than you love God?***

Week 20

Life is full of choices. Every character in this week's Quiet Time made choices. Those who chose evil brought incredible misery and suffering on themselves and the people around them. You can choose to be a Rehoboam or an Elijah–you make the choice. Have it your way!

Prayer Focus for this week:

**Q: The QUESTION - What is the writer saying?**

**A: The APPLICATION- How can I apply this to my life?**

Sunday 1 Kings 11:41-12:15

Q:

A:

Digging DEEPER

Solomon asked God for an understanding heart and God granted his request. Now, 40 years later, his son Rehoboam needed wisdom as well. Unfortunately, he only asked men for advice. He did not include God. He chose to follow the foolish counsel of his peers. Notice the contrast. The old men said in verse 7, be a servant, be accountable, and be a teacher. The young men gave the exact opposite advice and it turned out to be so evil that it resulted in division of the kingdom. Only two of the twelve tribes of Israel stayed with Rehoboam.

***Whose advice are you taking today? Are you seeking counsel of older people who have a history of walking with God, or are you seeking the advice of young people who are "doing their own thing?" Why not do what Solomon did and ask God for "understanding to discern judgment?"***

Life stEP

Monday 1 Kings 12:16-30

Q:

A:

**Digging DEEPER** Wrong decisions lead to wrong actions. Did you ever notice how little things can become huge? Rehoboam got the wrong advice from the wrong people and it started a revolution in Israel. There were twelve tribes in Israel that made up the nation. Ten of the tribes chose Jereboam to be their king and only two of the tribes stayed with Rehoboam in Jerusalem. Now there were two kings and both were evil. Jereboam set up false idols and the country took up arms getting ready to fight and kill their own brothers!

***What decisions do you have to make today? Even though they may seem small, do you realize that making the right decision today will result in great blessing later?***

**Life stEP**

Tuesday 1 Kings 13:1-10

Q:

A:

**Digging DEEPER** King Jeroboam was sinning against God by setting up idol worship which was in direct disobedience to the second commandment (Exodus 20:4). God was faithful to send a man of God to Bethel to rebuke Jeroboam. He told the king that Joash would be born and he would tear down the altar. This literally happened 360 years later (2 Kings 23:15)! This made Jeroboam so angry that he commanded his soldiers to grab the man of God. The rest of the story is a story of God's protection and a story of the courage it takes to do what is right, even when it is difficult.

***Do you have the courage to "go another way" (v. 10) like the man of God when he was tempted with money? Conviction is something for which you are willing to die. What are your scriptural convictions?***

**Life stEP**

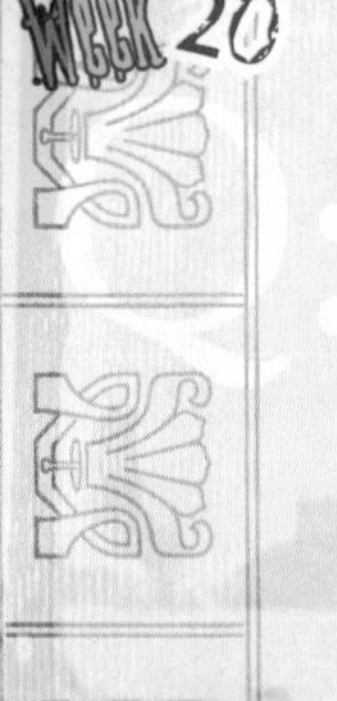

## Wednesday 1 Kings 13:11-25

**Digging Deeper**

Just because someone is religious, does not mean they are right? Right is right, and wrong is wrong, and God is always right! The man of God should have obeyed God. After all, God had spoken clearly. Now an old prophet in Bethel was willing to compromise by lying. He said that an angel told him to get the man of God to come back. Wrong choice! What could not be accomplished through the royal invitation was accomplished through religious compromise. (See what Galatians 1:8 has to say about this!) A lion had a great meal that day!

***What is God saying to you about compromising with false religions? Are you listening to any false gospels? Are you making your decisions based on what God reveals in His Word, the Bible?***

**Life stEP**

## Thursday 1 Kings 16:29-17:7

**Digging Deeper**

One evil king after another came to reign in the northern and southern kingdoms. The most evil one of all was Ahab, with a wife as evil (or perhaps more evil) as he was. With evil kings all around, God raises up His own man who would not compromise. He was a rugged man who was unafraid to tell the truth even when it was unpopular. His name was Elijah, the Tishbite. He was prepared to preach against Baal worship and let God provide his needs.

***With whom are you standing? Do you stand with God and the Bible? Elijah stood for right and obeyed God (1 Kings 17:5). Are you standing before God in a daily quiet time, and then obeying what God shows you from His Word?***

**Life stEP**

Friday 1 Kings 17:8-24



Q:

A:

Digging DEEPER Hush! It's quiet time… at least it was for Elijah. He was in a secluded place totally dependant on God. But then something happened; the brook Cherith which quenched his thirst, dried up! What's God up to? Before too long He would use Elijah to perform two miracles to prove Himself. He provided food for the prophet and for the widow woman and her son, but note the order – "Feed me first" is essentially what Elijah said. God always asks us to give to Him first when it comes to time and money. Then, later God raises her son from the dead (v. 22). There's always more than enough if God comes first!

***Would you trust God like the widow woman did? If we can't trust Him for our food, will we trust Him one day with our children? Have you trusted Jesus Christ with your soul?*** Life stEP

Saturday 1 Kings 18:1-16

Q:

A:

Digging DEEPER Can you believe that for three years Elijah was hiding at Cherith and Zeraphath? He was out of sight where no one could see him but God. Now he was coming out in public for the real test of his faith and character. Elijah is God's man, but Obadiah is a compromising believer. Obadiah was a person who wanted to love the Lord and love the world, too. Even though Obadiah had once taken a stand for the Lord earlier in life (v. 4), now he had lost his courage (v. 12).

***Do you want to serve God and the world at the same time? You know that it is impossible. Would you rather be an Elijah, or an Obadiah? Why not tell Jesus right now, "Lord, I am yours, all the way – 100%!"?***

## Week 21

"One man with God is a majority in any community" the old preacher said. Elijah went up against 450 false prophets, *and* Ahab and Jezebel. I guess you know who won. Stay tuned for one of the biggest battles and victories in Scripture!

Prayer Focus for this week:

**Q: The QUESTION - What is the writer saying?**

**A: The APPLICATION- How can I apply this to my life?**

Sunday 1 Kings 18:17-29

Q:

A:

Digging DEEPER

During strong opposition, have you ever taken a stand for something that is right? If you have, you know how Elijah felt when he stood alone against King Ahab. Ahab blamed Elijah the prophet for the trouble in Israel. Elijah let him know that the trouble (presumably the three-year drought and famine) was caused by his wickedness in worshiping the false god, Baal. Elijah was courageous in the face of evil and he called for a showdown. It was 450 false prophets against one man who was willing to stand alone with God.

***What about you, are you willing to stand against what is wrong, even if you have to stand alone? Are you spending time alone with God so that you can walk with God like Elijah did?***

Life stEP

Monday 1 Kings 18:30-40

Q:

A:

**Digging Deeper**

Sixty-three words in prayer from Elijah brought down the fire of God. Look at Elijah's words (vv. 36-37) and you will see how a man that walks with God prays. He prayed that God would be known for Who He truly is. He prayed that it would be known that he was doing what God commanded him to do. He prayed that the people would be turned back to God. God answered that humble prayer and the fire of God fell and burned up the sacrifice. The stones of the altar were consumed as well as licking up the twelve barrels of water poured on the altar!

***Want to pray like Elijah and have power with God like he did? You can start by being fully surrendered to God. It continues by walking with God on a daily basis, just like you are doing now in your daily quiet time with God.***

Life stEP

Tuesday 1 Kings 18:41-19:7

Q:

A:

**Digging Deeper**

Did you ever have a great week at camp or a great time on a mission trip, only to come back home and get discouraged? Elijah just had three incredible victories. God had proven Himself by burning his offering on the altar. He had slain 450 prophets of Baal, and God had answered his prayer right in front of wicked King Ahab by causing it to rain after three years of drought. Often, after a victory, discouragement comes. Elijah became fearful of wicked Jezebel who threatened his life. He felt like a failure and he probably was just plain worn out. God would refresh him in a quiet, out-of-the-way place in the wilderness.

***Don't be surprised if you get discouraged after God does something great in your life. Have you considered taking some time to rest and gain new strength from God?***

Wednesday 1 Kings 19:8-21

God had an answer for Elijah's discouragement, "Go stand…before the Lord" (v. 11). One of the greatest lessons in the Christian life is learning how to hear the voice of God. It wasn't in the wind and earthquake, or fire, but God's voice was a still, small voice. God speaks to us in our hearts through His Word. When Elijah took time to listen to God, He told him all that he needed to know. God told Elijah that he was not the only one standing for Him and that there were 7,000 other people who had not bowed their knee to Baal. He also told him to anoint two kings and to anoint Elisha to be a prophet in his place.

***What are you waiting for? Do you expect to hear God speak in some loud, spectacular way? What is He saying to your heart as you read His Word? Your quiet time is the place where God's voice can be heard.***

Life stEP

Thursday 1 Kings 21:1-16

Covetousness is just a word, so what does it have to do with me anyway? Words have meaning and the meaning of the word is ugly. "Thou shalt not covet" is the tenth commandment (Exodus 20:17). Paul called it "lust." Mark said it comes from the heart and defiles a person. Ahab shows what it means to covet something. He wants Naboth's vineyard so badly that he allows his evil wife to have Nabal murdered. Covetousness is much more than just wanting something you don't have, it means that you are willing to sin to get it. Any time we are willing to sin to get something, we have become covetous, just like Ahab.

***Are you focused on the temporary things of this world? Why not refocus your attention on God and His promises? This is the way to true contentment.***

Life stEP

Friday 1 Kings 21:17-29

Q:

A:

Digging DEEPER God will ultimately judge all sin, but He prefers to show grace. 2 Peter 3:9 tells us that God is longsuffering – He literally *suffers a long time with us and is patient.* His timing is not always the same as ours. When we read this story, we want to see God judge wicked Ahab immediately, but God often surprises us with His willingness to withhold His judgment. He is waiting for us to ask forgiveness and repent of our sins. Elijah's announcement (v. 21) caused Ahab to repent (v. 27) and caused God to withhold His judgment (v. 20).

***Can you see how quickly God is willing to forgive us for our sins? 1 John 1:9 says that God is faithful and just to forgive us of our sins, if we will only confess them to Him. Do you need forgiveness today? Why not ask, and know that He hears and answers our prayers – immediately!*** Life stEP

Saturday 1 Kings 22:29-40

Q:

A:

Digging DEEPER You've probably never heard of him, but Micaiah, the prophet, was a true man of God. His stand for God cost him his life. On the other hand, Ahab was intent on destroying himself. Although he was repentant at one point which delayed God's judgment, we now see him ignoring all warnings and running to his death. Do you think the arrow that pierced his armor was merely "random" (v. 34)? Do you believe that the exact place where Ahab's chariot was washed out (compare 21:19 with 22:38) was just by accident? We can see that God is sovereign – He is the Ruler and He is in control!

***What is happening in your life today? Do you think that everything is just random or accidental? Why not look for God's sovereign hand in all your circumstances today?***

Week 22

Fire from heaven, a flaming chariot, a mantle parting a river, empty oil pots miraculously filled, a miracle birth, and a dead boy raised – is your life this exciting? The lives of Elijah and Elisha were this exciting and much more. Who knows what God may do in your life as you learn to walk with Him this week?

Prayer Focus for this week:

Q: The QUESTION - What is the writer saying?

A: The APPLICATION- How can I apply this to my life?

Sunday 2 Kings 1:1-18

Q:

A:

Digging DEEPER

Ahaziah, the son of Ahab, became king in Israel after his father's death. Sadly, he only lived two years because of his evil ways. He was an idol worshipper in direct opposition to God's clear command and turned to the prophets of Baal in Ekron. In contrast, Elijah was a man of God and his character was well known to the king. His power from God was proven when he called fire down from heaven on two groups of 50 soldiers. Eventually, Elijah came and pronounced God's judgment on Ahaziah face to face. James and John asked Jesus for the same power that Elijah had. His answer is the difference between law and grace.

*Why not ask God for His power today; not the power to destroy, but the power to win men to Christ? Power to win souls to Jesus Christ comes from God and His Word alone.*

Life stEP

Monday 2 Kings 2:1-11

Q:

A:

**Digging DEEPER** God had a new prophet that would replace Elijah. His name was Elisha. Elijah was to be caught up (raptured away) from the earth and Elisha wanted to be there and witness it. It is a picture of the Rapture that all believers are expecting! Elisha was a real man's man. He knew who to hang out with and what to ask for. He was in a harness pulling with twelve yoke of oxen when Elijah got called away. His service on earth ended in God's presence. Because Elisha was present and watching, he received a double portion of Elijah's spirit (vv. 9-10) just like he was told.

***You are known by your friends. Who are you hanging out with? Do you have a godly person that is older than you that you are seeking out for godly counsel?*** **Life stEP**

Tuesday 2 Kings 2:12-22

Q:

A:

**Digging DEEPER** Did you ever hear about the mantle of leadership being passed from one person to another? Often we hear about it in large corporations, in Congress, or when we get a new president. Today's Quiet Time is where this idea started. Elijah had been the great, powerful leader of God's people, and now he was raptured into the very presence of God. The mantle of leadership has fallen to a new man, Elisha, whom God has prepared for this very task. He immediately takes up Elijah's mantle and uses it to part the waters of Jordan and shortly thereafter, turns poisoned water into drinkable water.

***God has a prepared place for a prepared person. Your quiet time will prepare you for future service. Are you being faithful?*** **Life stEP**

Wednesday 2 Kings 4:1-17

The next two miracles tell us that He cares for young and old, rich and poor. He cares for us all. The first woman was the widow of a seminary student. Evidently, her husband had died unexpectedly and the creditors, according to the law (Leviticus 25:39), were coming to take her sons away to work and pay off the bills. Elisha gives her a way out through faith! Secondly, a great woman and her husband desired to help Elisha. Perhaps they were rich, but more likely, they were rich in faith. They provided a "prophet's chamber" for Elisha and Gehazi, his servant, to stay in when they traveled. Then Elisha announced that she was to have a child, one of the greatest miracles in the Old Testament.

***Do you recognize the great men and women of God around you in the world today? Are you asking their advice and following their lead?***

Life stEP

Thursday 2 Kings 4:18-37

God had given the Shunammite woman and her husband a son. He was an extra special blessing from the Lord. Now, unexpectedly, he dies from sunstroke. This mother goes into action and leaves to find Elisha. Notice how she said, "It is well" all along the way. Truly, it was well with her soul even though she was in a terrible crisis. God honored her faith and brought her son back to life. We know that Romans 8:28 says that all things work together for good to those who love God. Through faith, it would have been well with her even if the child had not been raised from the dead. That's having confidence in God!

***How's your prayer life? Is there any unconfessed sin that would hinder your prayers? What are you asking God for? Can you expect to get it?***

Life stEP

Friday 2 Kings 4:38-44



Q:

A:

Digging DEEPER God uses different people in different ways. At Mount Carmel, Elijah called down fire from heaven. God uses Elisha for a smaller miracle here to save the school of prophets from food poisoning. The school of prophets that Elijah started was having a meal. Someone found a wild gourd and ground it up in the pot. Elisha told the people what to do to stop the poisoning of the student body, "…bring meal…and cast it into the pot." In Leviticus, meal is a type of the Lord, and when the Lord enters, death leaves and life comes! Elisha also miraculously fed 100 men in verses 42-44. God honors His prophet and uses him to help His people.

*Find a great man or woman who walks with the Lord and learn the secrets of their spiritual walk. Then seek to duplicate these traits in your life.*

Life stEP

Saturday 2 Kings 5:1-16

Q:

A:

Digging DEEPER The story of Naaman is a beautiful picture of salvation. Naaman was a Syrian, an enemy of the people of Israel, yet God used a slave girl to get the message of healing to this general. When he finally got to Elisha, he was told to go dip seven times in the Jordan River. This was an insult to a man with so much wealth, yet his money and position (works) could not buy a cure for his incurable disease of leprosy. Leprosy is likened to sin; we have to come in humility and be saved God's way and that's the way of the Cross.

***Do you know someone like Naaman who has an incurable disease (sin)? If God can use the simple testimony of a slave girl, surely He can use you. Will you be His witness today?***

Life stEP

Week 23

Hollywood can't write movie scripts any better than what you'll read this week. How about a man who turns whiter than snow, or an axe head that swims, or flying chariots of fire, streaking armies, or a queen with her face painted thrown out of the palace window! These stories are just ahead… read and heed!

Prayer Focus for this week:

**Q: The QUESTION - What is the writer saying?**

**A: The APPLICATION- How can I apply this to my life?**

Sunday 2 Kings 5:17-27

Q:

A:

Digging DEEPER

"…But he was a leper" (v. 1) would be the most terrifying thing a person could hear about himself. It's like saying "…you have *AIDS*!" It's a death sentence. Naaman had been cured, but now Gehazi, Elisha's servant, would be stricken with the same disease. Unless God tells us specifically, we can never know the cause of disease. In Naaman's case, it was for the glory of God. In Gehazi's case, it was in judgment for his covetousness. How sad for Gehazi to serve Elisha faithfully and observe the power of God flowing through Elisha's life, and then fall into the sin of covetousness. Things never satisfy. Remember, *Thou shalt not covet* is the last of the Ten Commandments (Exodus 20:17)!

***Getting into His presence will help us from going after the world's presents. What are you longing for today?***

Monday 2 Kings 6:1-7

Q:

A:

Digging DEEPER

Hudson Taylor, the great missionary to China, once said, "God's work, done in God's way, will never lack God's supply." The students at Elisha's school of prophets needed a bigger building. They borrowed an axe and went to work cutting down trees with which to build. Somehow the axe head flew off into the water: they had a crisis. Elisha performed another miracle by cutting down a stick and casting it in the water where the axe head had gone in. The iron axe head floated to the top of the water. Now the students could go back to work to build their dormitory! Paul said, "I can do all things through Christ which strengtheneth me." We must have God's power to get His work done in His way!

Life stEP

***Do you need God's power in your life today? Why not admit your need and watch the iron (of God's strength) swim and enable you to serve Him.***

Tuesday 2 Kings 6:8-23

Q:

A:

It is amazing the work that God does behind the scenes and in the hearts of people whom we least expect. There was an information leak from the palace bedroom of the King of Syria. The servants of the king knew that it wasn't them who were leaking his battle secrets, but that God was telling the battle plans to the man of God, Elisha! As if that was not enough, the King of Syria set himself up for another lesson about God's power and might. When he sent a host of soldiers and chariots to intimidate Elisha, he himself was surrounded by an army of angels! We need to pray that God would open our eyes to see His great protection that surrounds us when we live for Him.

***Have you thanked God for His power and protection today? Why not do it now and remember that He is with you throughout the day!***

Wednesday 2 Kings 6:24-33

When we get into trouble, we naturally want to blame someone else for it, but sometimes we need to look at ourselves first to see if the trouble is with us. Israel was in total rebellion against God. Now, the judgment of God was coming on them just as it had been prophesied. The city of Samaria was surrounded by the enemy's army. God's people, who were inside, were starving to death. The trouble was brought on by their sin, but the king decided to blame the prophet Elisha. Notice how the prophet was at peace when he was threatened. The king finally realized that the trouble had come from the Lord. Isn't it interesting how the ungodly try to blame believers for their problems?

***Are you building your faith by studying His Word? Why not try to find some additional time to read the Bible again today!***

Thursday 2 Kings 7:1-11

"Why sit we here until we die?" This is a great motivating question for any Christian to ask. We could take this question of the lepers and move into action. God has given us an awesome job to do – to take the Gospel to the ends of the earth (Matthew 28:19-20). This story is another amazing chapter in Elisha's life. You recall from chapter 6 that Samaria was starving. Now, Elisha tells the king that within 24 hours the high cost of food (2 Kings 6:25) would be reduced to almost nothing. The four lepers got in on an awesome blessing when they decided to move out of the city. Thankfully, they decided to share what they had received. This is another amazing Bible story with wonderful lessons for us today.

***Are you sitting and dying instead of standing and serving the Lord? Are you sharing the wonderful "good tidings" (v. 9) of the Gospel?***

Life
stEP

Friday 2 Kings 7:12-20

Q:

A:

Digging DEEPER Who are you listening to? Elisha had a proven track record and time after time we have been reading how God was answering his prayers and proving his words to be true. We need to stay close to those people who walk with God and take His Word as their guide. The king doubted the good news and was proven wrong. The king's lord doubted the word of Elisha and died in the stampede to get cheap food. God has His way of honoring His Word and His people. What a miraculous provision of God! This is the grace of God. We do not expect, nor do we deserve it, yet God, in His goodness, continually pours it out on us.

*Are you experiencing the blessings of God as you take Him at His Word? Or are you missing all His promises because of unbelief?*

Life stEP

Saturday 2 Kings 9:1-10, 30-37

Q:

A:

Digging DEEPER God's will shall come to pass just as it is written. Payday is coming for wicked Jezebel. What Elijah predicted 15 years before in 1 Kings 21:23 is about to come to pass. Jehu was anointed as king and would be the instrument for Jezebel's destruction. In verse 30 she painted her face and taunted him as he entered the city. Jehu commands that she be thrown down from her elevated place. She is killed and the dogs eat her flesh. It is a brutal end to an unrepentant sinner. Soon the prophecy of Revelation 2:20 will be fulfilled as the judgment of Jezebel was. God always has the last word.

*The sowing and reaping principle is always in effect – if you sow to the flesh, you will reap corruption. If you sow to the spirit, you will reap life everlasting (Galatians 6:7-9). What are you sowing today?*

Week 24

These final chapters are power-packed! Elisha dies, but his power goes on. Israel is judged, yet God proves faithful 2,000 years later. God answers one of the greatest prayers in the Bible. Find out about God's "precious things." See what a country is like when the Bible is lost for 50 years! Dig into it this week!

Prayer Focus for this week:

**Q: The QUESTION - What is the writer saying?**

**A: The APPLICATION- How can I apply this to my life?**

Sunday 2 Kings 13:14-21

Q:

A:

Digging DEEPER

Elisha is faithful to the very end of his life. King Joash, the grandson of Jehu, comes to see Elisha on his deathbed. Joash speaks of the chariots of Israel and how a double portion of Elijah's power had fallen on Elisha. Now, Elisha has one final blessing for Israel and one strange miracle. He told Joash to shoot five arrows. Unfortunately, by shooting only three he limited his victories over Syria to just three. The final miracle is in verse 21 when a dead man comes back to life after being lowered into Elisha's grave and touching his bones. Even Elisha's dead bones had power! Perhaps God was showing Israel that he would raise them back to life one day, as He will do during the Tribulation period.

***Are you limiting God by only partially obeying Him? He is already the Lord of the universe; why not let Him rule in your heart and life today?***

Life stEP

Monday 2 Kings 17:6-23

Q:

A:

**Digging DEEPER** When God speaks, He doesn't stutter! God's Word is clear. God's people were to worship God alone and obey His command. Nevertheless, Israel was determined to disobey and walk in their sinful ways. Therefore, they have never recovered from the captivity described here. A whole array of wicked sins are mentioned. There were some good kings in Judah, but there were no good kings in Israel. One day, when the church is completed and raptured, Israel's blindness will cease and God will restore Israel (Romans 11:25).

*Joshua said "Choose you this day whom ye will serve…" (Joshua 24:15). What is your choice today? Are you wrestling between allegiance to Jesus Christ and allegiance to the world (1 John 2:15-17)? Choose to do the will of God in your life today.* **Life stEP**

Tuesday 2 Kings 17:24-41

Q:

A:

**Digging DEEPER** The woman at the well in John 4 is the direct descendent of the Samaritans. They were the result of intermarriage of God's people with the godless people of Samaria. When you take a little of this religion and a little of that religion and make up your own, it's called *syncretism.* The world is full of that kind of religion today. You probably know a lot of people who say, "Everybody's right, nobody's wrong, all religions are good, and we all serve the same god!" Although it sounds familiar, Jesus didn't agree with it (John 14:6, Acts 4:12 and Matthew 6:24)! How sad that Israel feared God on one hand, but served its own gods on the other (vv. 33, 41).

*Are you absolutely convinced that Jesus Christ is the only way to heaven? Who can you share this Good News with today?*

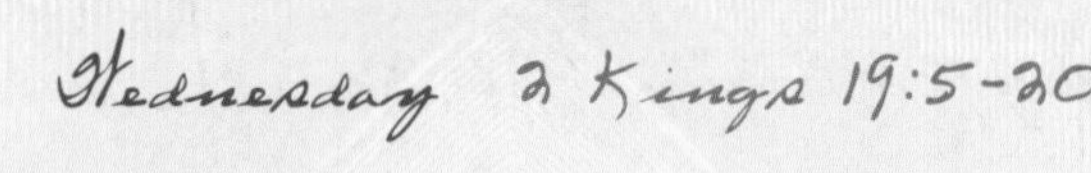


Digging DEEPER

As Christians, we are in a battle with Satan and all his evil forces. King Hezekiah was in a life and death battle with Sennacherib, King of Assyria. He had an evil spokesman named Rab-Shakeh. This man lied and misrepresented God. Hezekiah took the threatening letter he received and "spread it before the Lord." God promised to defeat the enemy so that all the earth would know that He was the Lord God! Now, God was going to have His say with these devil-inspired enemies of God. One day "…every knee should bow… and …every tongue should confess that Jesus Christ is Lord, to the glory of God the Father" (Philippians 2:10-11).

Life stEP

***Isn't it great knowing you are on the winning team? With God's help, what do you dare to pray for and what victory will you claim today?***

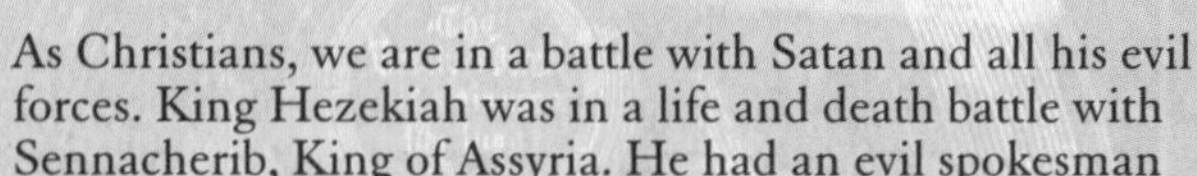

God heard the prayer of Hezekiah. Sennacherib's army of 185,000 was all killed by one angel in one night. Evil Sennacherib was then murdered by his own sons while worshiping his god. Now, King Hezekiah becomes sick and God tells him he is going to die. In this amazing story, Hezekiah chose not to accept the counsel of God that he was to die, but rather requested that he continue to live. Every believer has a right to offer his prayers to God. God, in His grace, heals him and gives him 15 more years. Sadly, Hezekiah backslides and falls into sin during this period, but ultimately repents. One good thing came about through this extension of life: Josiah, a great king, was born.

***Prayer is one of the greatest blessings the child of God has. Are you taking advantage of it? What have you prayed for today?***

Friday 2 Kings 20:12-21

Q:

A:

**Digging DEEPER** In time of war, booby traps are commonly used. They are used to secretly wound or kill the enemy. Hezekiah was a great king. He restored the temple and led a great revival in Jerusalem. He survived the invasion by Sennacherib. He even survived the crisis of sickness and then God gave him 15 more years to live. But, he failed the test of prosperity and became proud of all that God had done for him. In his arrogance, he showed off all the "precious things" in the temple to the Babylonian enemy. Isaiah pronounced the judgment of God on Hezekiah's foolishness by telling him that all these treasures would one day be carried off to Babylon. This occurred about 100 years later. Pride is enemy #1.

*Pride will allow Satan to steal your joy and blessings. Guard your heart and learn to give God the honor and glory. Why not offer praise to Him now!* **Life stEP**

Saturday 2 Kings 22:3-10; 23:1-3

Q:

A:

**Digging DEEPER** It has now been 275 years since the man of God prophesied Josiah's birth. Now, the young eight-year-old king begins his reign (2 Kings 22:1). When he was 16 years old, his heart began to seek after God. At age 20, he tore down the altars in Israel. However, when Josiah was 26, the most amazing thing happened. While cleaning out the temple after 50+ years of neglect, they made a startling discovery, "I have found the book of the law…" (2 Kings 22:8). This started a great revival. Revival always involves the reading of God's Word. The opposite is also true; when we neglect the Word, we can expect sin and bondage,

*How do you see the Word of God? As you read His Word today, let it be the joy and rejoicing of your heart. Let God's Word change you like it did Josiah and all Jerusalem! The Word of God is still a GREAT discovery!*

Week 25

Do you ever wish you could just start over? You can as we start this new gospel. We'll get a new perspective on who Jesus is, and how He affected those around Him. This week we will learn about Jesus' first miracles and more about His deity. We can start fresh by asking "Who is this Jesus?"

Prayer Focus for this week:

**Q: The QUESTION - What is the writer saying?**

**A: The APPLICATION- How can I apply this to my life?**

Sunday John 1:1-14

Q:

A:

Digging DEEPER

When you read "In the beginning," what was the first thing you thought of? Genesis 1:1, of course. God was already there when human history was first recorded. This passage explains that Jesus was the Creator of the world. John's Gospel presents Jesus in all His deity. He uses the terms *Word, Life,* and *Light* to reveal that Jesus is God. Then, to those who receive Him (v. 12), He gave the power (right) to become "sons of God." Do you find that amazing? We can become children of the Almighty God, by His will, of course, not ours (v. 13).

*Are you a child of God? If you are not sure, talk to a leader or friend who can show you how. What are you willing to do for the Creator, who wants to call you His Child? Write down one thing and work on it this week.*

Life stEP

Monday John 1:15-28

Q:

A:

**Digging DEEPER** Do you like riddles? There are many of them in Scripture. They make us think deeper than we normally think. The Apostle John, the author of this book, lets us see into the ministry and message of John the Baptist. People sent by the Pharisees asked him who he was. The Pharisees probably felt threatened by his ministry. John the Baptist responded with a riddle. He denied being the Messiah, Elijah, or the prophet but simply said he was *the voice* (Isaiah 40:3). His message clearly declares Christ's pre-existence as the Son of God and that His ministry would be full of grace and truth.

***Think deeply about what John says about Jesus Christ. Who do people see in your ministry and message? Choose one action this week that enables you to share the Gospel with at least one other person.***

**Life stEP**

Tuesday John 1:29-42

Q:

A:

**Digging DEEPER** Have you ever known something and just couldn't keep it a secret? Maybe someone famous was coming to town and you were going to meet him. You would want everyone to know. That is the way John the Baptist is in these verses. In a special way, God revealed to him who Jesus was. John wasn't worried when his own followers left him to follow Jesus. If fact, he was happy (John 3:30). His follower Andrew, who later became one of Jesus' disciples, brought his brother Simon to meet Jesus claiming He was the Messiah. Andrew is known for introducing many people to Jesus (John 6:8-9; 12:22).

***Do you know how to take another person through the Scriptures to show him that Jesus is God? Pray and ask God to reveal one person to you who you can introduce to Jesus Christ this week.***

**Life stEP**

Wednesday John 1:43-51

Q:

A:

Digging Deeper

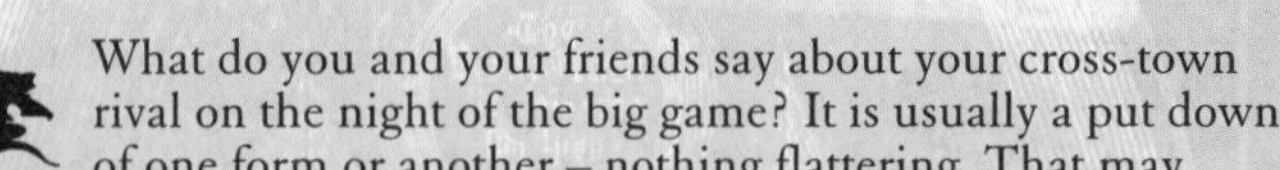

What do you and your friends say about your cross-town rival on the night of the big game? It is usually a put down of one form or another – nothing flattering. That may have been how Nathanael considered the people from Nazareth. What a great example we see in Philip who, like Andrew, brought his friend Nathanael to meet Jesus. We don't know exactly what Nathanael was doing under the fig tree. Some scholars think he was meditating on Old Testament Scripture or praying. It is clear that he quickly changed his mind about Jesus when Jesus said He saw him under the fig tree.

***What have you done about the person you asked God to reveal to you yesterday? Find a way today to talk to that person about Jesus.***

Thursday John 2:1-12

Q:

A:

Do you enjoy weddings? Most girls love them while most guys tolerate them. They are joyous occasions where the guests come to celebrate and encourage the new couple. The fact that Jesus chose a wedding to perform His first miracle shows us that He wasn't looking for recognition. If He were, wouldn't He perform the miracle in the temple or another public place with many people as witnesses? Also, look closely at what He did. He bypassed the whole process of growing the grapes and making them into wine. This proves His ability to create with the appearance of age. This is the first of seven signs (miracles) that John records to convince us to believe in the Lord Jesus Christ and His deity.

***What do you think about Jesus now? Write down one thing God taught you in today's passage and meditate on it.***

Friday John 2:13-25

Q:

A:

Digging DEEPER If you were in the temple that day, who would you be? Would you be a merchant, selling animals to those coming to make sacrifices for Passover? Maybe you'd be a banker *helping* people change their money to be able to pay for things. Both groups were greedy in their dealings and were very upset when this *new guy* came in disrupting things. Perhaps you'd be one of the masses there to celebrate Passover, puzzled about what was going on, but enjoying the miracles. Even the disciples were a little confused. They were still learning who this Jesus was. They would remember these things after the Resurrection and it would strengthen their faith (John 12:16).

***Whom do you relate to in today's passage? What is one thing you can do today to become a better disciple of Jesus? Do it.*** Life stEP

Saturday John 3:1-12

Q:

A:

Digging DEEPER If you were a recognized religious authority, a teacher of the law, and part of the Sanhedrin, why would you want to speak privately with Jesus after dark? Because, you are supposed to be the religious expert and you don't want others to see you asking questions. Jesus patiently explained the spiritual second birth to Nicodemus, illustrating it with the wind. John mentions Nicodemus three times in this Gospel so we can witness the progression of his faith. It is hard to believe that the first person to hear John 3:16 (from the Lord Himself) does not respond positively. We are not told what happens, but in John 7:50 Nicodemus defends Jesus against charges made by the Sanhedrin. Then, in John 19:38-39, Nicodemus stands with Joseph to care for Jesus' body after the Crucifixion.

***Where are you in your progression of faith? Take the next step!***

Week 28

Do people know that you are a disciple of Jesus Christ because of your love for others and your faithfulness in His Word? This week you will find people who knew Scripture, knew their place, and took God at His Word. You'll see Jesus ignoring social codes and caring for people that others hated.

Prayer Focus for this week:

**Q: The QUESTION - What is the writer saying?**

**A: The APPLICATION- How can I apply this to my life?**

Sunday John 3:13-24

Q:

A:

Digging DEEPER

How much of the Old Testament do you know? Jesus understood that Nicodemus knew the Old Testament forward and backward. Therefore, He related the Exodus story in Numbers 21 to him. Read it. It's about complaining, rebellion, death, snakes, and how to survive! In the end, the people were required to believe and look at something in faith. Jesus relates this to His (then) coming sacrifice on the cross as an example of how future generations will have to look forward in faith to the Cross for salvation. Today we look back to the Cross and must believe and receive by faith what Jesus has already provided.

*Look back and truly thank Jesus for all He did for you on the Cross? Read the passage in Numbers 21 and see how all of Scripture works together, even when written hundreds of years apart.*

Life stEP

Monday John 3:25-36

Q:

A:

**Digging Deeper** What are you best at – either athletically or academically? Imagine you held the world record in that activity. What happens next? After several years, someone else will come along and break your record. Are you sad? Of course not. John the Baptist was probably one of the greatest men who ever lived. However, he knew who he was in comparison to the Lord Jesus Christ. Jesus was from heaven and, by nature, was superior to him. God used John (and is still using him) to point many to Jesus. John was glad when more people followed Jesus than him. In verse 36, John gives a clear statement as to what it means to be saved. Reread it. Make sure you fully understand it. If you do, share it with someone.

***Pointing people to Jesus is the thing that matters most in life. Whom will you point to the Lord Jesus Christ today?***

**Life stEP**

Tuesday John 4:1-15

Q:

A:

**Digging Deeper** Jesus was not *politically correct* in His day. Most Jewish people did not associate with Samaritans because they were considered half-breeds. Also, in that culture, men didn't talk to women they didn't know. Jesus ignored the social code of His day and asked this woman for a drink of water. Why? We know from the miracles He's already performed that He could have provided for Himself. However, He knew this woman couldn't. She needed what only He could provide. Note that He used something she could relate to, *water*, to introduce and explain spiritual truth to her. Notice she was interested in hearing more.

***What can you use to explain spiritual truth to someone? Ask the Lord to give you an opportunity today to share His truth with that person.***

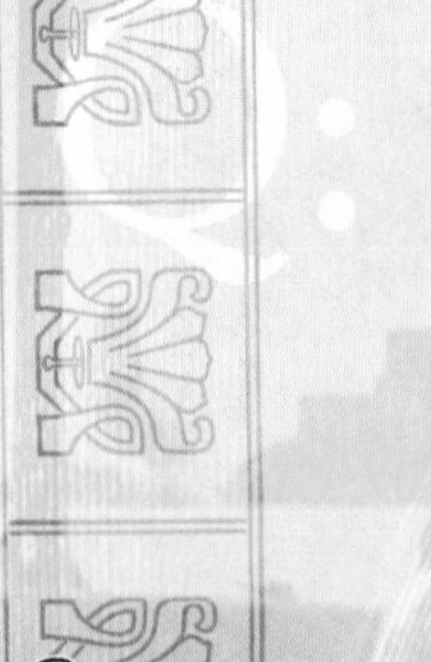


Wednesday John 4:16-30

Digging DEEPER When someone is telling you something that you don't want to hear, what do you do? Changing the subject is a popular tactic. The Samaritan woman took that option when she brought up the issue of where to worship (which was a major point of contention between the Jews and Samaritans). Jesus reveals that it is not the location but the heart attitude with which you come to God (Psalm 24:4). What do you think the people of the town thought when the woman returned claiming that a Man told her everything she'd done? She then wondered if this One could be the Messiah.

***Is there a group of people you wouldn't approach with the Gospel? Get over it! Where do you worship? You can worship right now, where you are!***

Thursday John 4:31-42

Do you live on a farm? Have you ever planted a garden? If you have, you know that when it's time for harvest it is crucial to get the crop in quickly before it rains. That is what Jesus is trying to get the disciples to consider. Instead, they worried about food as the people from the town were coming out to see Him. Jesus shares another principle with them that compares the known (or natural) with the spiritual. With the Gospel not everyone gets to do the harvesting. Some will plant, some will water, some will cultivate, and others will bring in the harvest. In this case, the disciples got to do the harvesting.

***Are you willing to skip a meal to share the Gospel with someone? Are you planting, watering, cultivating, or harvesting the Gospel today?***

Life stEP

Friday John 4:43-54

Q:

A:

Digging Deeper Are you willing to take God at His word? How often have we seen God work in a mysterious way then later begin to second guess or explain it away? This is very easy to do and it is one of Satan's favorite tools. He wants to get the focus of our minds away from our Almighty God and onto something else. Notice the man didn't appeal to his royal position or defend himself in light of Jesus' charge of wanting to see a sign, but humbly, in faith, appealed to Jesus to save his dying son. What a demonstration of Jesus' power! Cana was approximately 20 miles from Capernaum. We see that Jesus was as capable of healing the child from a distance as He was standing at his bedside.

*Take God at His word. Claim by faith something God has told you in His Word. Consider witnessing, memory work, truthfulness, and faithfulness to name a few, and do it.* Life stEP

Saturday John 5:1-14

Q:

A:

Digging Deeper How many people do you know who cling to a false hope or a false religion built on the traditions of men rather than the Word of God? It is popular today to believe in angels. It's interesting to observe that in today's passage, an angel was supposed to stir the water of the pool and the next person in was believed to be healed. Note: it didn't say any person ever was healed. This type of healing is not found anywhere else in Scripture. Jesus had compassion on this one man and gave him a command, which he followed. The man was clear in his testimony to the Jews as to why he was disobeying a Sabbath law. The one who healed him from his disease of 38 years had told him to do it. Wouldn't you?

*Do what Jesus has told you to do. Share the truth; be a light to someone living in darkness. Obey the Word God has spoken to your heart.*

Week 27

Do you always follow the rules? It's interesting to notice that Jesus didn't always follow man's rules. Being God, He had a good reason. He is the Ruler. This week we'll get a detailed look at Jesus feeding the 5000 and how the people wanted to follow rules and be cared for physically but not spiritually.

Prayer Focus for this week:

**Q: The QUESTION - What is the writer saying?**

**A: The APPLICATION- How can I apply this to my life?**

Sunday John 5:15-27

Q:

A:

Digging Deeper

Have you ever played a game with someone who didn't follow the rules? It's irritating, isn't it? That's what the Pharisees thought about Jesus. He wasn't following the rules that had been laid out by the *religious rulers* over centuries. If only they knew to Whom they were talking. Jesus healed a man on the Sabbath, and claimed to be equal with God. Jesus Christ also declared His commitment to doing the Father's will, and made it clear that one cannot have a valid faith in God the Father apart from a faith in Jesus, the Son of God. The key is a relationship with the Ruler, not just obedience to the rules.

***Whose rules are you following? What is one thing you can do today to show your love and commitment to Him?***

Life stEP

Monday John 5:28-38

Q:

A:

**Digging Deeper** What do you do when you want to prove a point to someone? You can argue the points yourself, but it's always impressive to bring in other witnesses to verify what you're saying. Jesus presents the Jews with five witnesses to His claim of deity. He was the first witness as to who He was. Second, John the Baptist bore witness. Jesus' miracles were third. When John the Baptist doubted in prison, Jesus let His works speak to assure John that He really was the Messiah. His Father was the fourth witness at His baptism, transfiguration, and Triumphal Entry. The fifth witness is Scripture (vv. 39-48).

**Life Step** ***Are you a witness for the Lord Jesus? Share what the Lord has recently done for you, or is teaching you in your quiet time, with at least one person.***

Tuesday John 5:39-47

Q:

A:

**Digging Deeper** Have you ever thought you were doing something the right way, only to find out later that you weren't? It could be embarrassing but usually not life-threatening. However, in the case of these religious leaders, it threatened their eternal destiny. They thought themselves to be experts in the Scripture, especially the Law of Moses (the first five books of the Old Testament). They thought that by strictly observing the law (as it was handed down and added to) they were assured of salvation. Can you imagine their shock when Jesus stated that Moses wrote of Him and the religious leaders didn't realize what He was talking about?

**Life Step** ***Do you have a relationship with the Ruler or are you strictly obeying a set of rules? The difference is where you will spend eternity.***

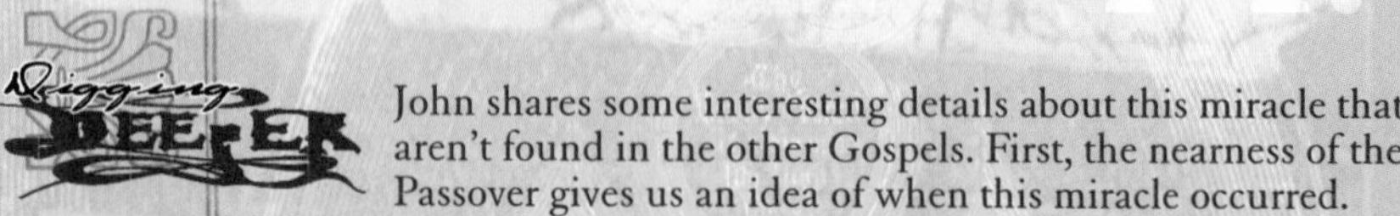

Digging DEEPER

John shares some interesting details about this miracle that aren't found in the other Gospels. First, the nearness of the Passover gives us an idea of when this miracle occurred. The testing of Philip is the second detail. Third, the bread was barley, which was coarse, cheap bread. Fourth, Andrew brings someone else to Jesus. Everyone got all they wanted to eat and Jesus asked for all the scraps to be gathered. It's interesting that there were 12 baskets and 12 disciples.

***Do you think this was a lesson on God's abundant supply? There are a number of other things we can consider, like the wording found in verse 12 compared with John 3:16; 6:39; 10:28; 18:9? Check them out. Write down one thing you learned today? Share it with someone.***

Life stEP

Thursday John 6:15-27

Digging DEEPER

What happens when someone claims to have seen a miracle? People flock to see and be a part of it, too. That is what happened here. Thousands of people got a free meal and hoped they could get another. That wasn't Jesus' purpose in doing it. The miracles Jesus performed were to show His deity (that He was the Son of God) but people focused only on their physical needs and not their spiritual needs. Jesus went to the mountain to pray. Then he came to the disciples walking on the water. This demonstrated His power over creation and His ability to surpass the physical limitations that bind mankind.

***What is your motivation in following God? What miracles (changes in lives) have you seen Jesus do lately? Share them with someone who needs encouragement.***

Life stEP

Friday John 6:28-40

Q:

A:

When we were little children, it was important to learn how to please our parents. Likewise, the people around Jesus wanted to know what they should do to please God. *Believe in Him* is the simple answer, but the people weren't content with that. They wanted another sign like Moses who fed the people manna for 40 years or some other sign that He was the Messiah. Jesus replied with the first of seven *I Am* statements claiming the name that God used to make Himself known to His chosen people (Exodus 3). Here He states that He is the *bread of life.* This referred to His latest miracle of feeding the 5000 and the conversation about Moses supplying bread (manna) in the wilderness.

***What can you do today to please God? Is Jesus your Bread of Life?*** Life stEP

Saturday John 6:41-58

Q:

A:

Digging Deeper

Have you ever been in a conversation where you were talking about one thing, but realized the other person was talking about something else? You were using the same words only they meant something different to each of you. The people wanted Jesus to throw off the oppression of Rome and meet their physical needs. They were not interested in His spiritual program. In the Gospels Jesus spoke in parables which often confused His casual followers. Therefore, when He presented Himself as the Bread of Life, which brings eternal life, they took it literally instead of spiritually. This passage speaks of spiritually consuming Him, the bread of life, by believing in Him as the Son of God.

***What must you do to satisfy your soul's need for the Bread of Life?***

Week 28

Do people know that you are a disciple of Jesus Christ because of your love for others and because you have continued in His Word? This week we'll see confused people trying to figure out just who this Jesus is. Jesus teaches spiritual truth to those who listen closely and simply believe. Will you?

Prayer Focus for this week:

**Q: The QUESTION - What is the writer saying?**
**A: The APPLICATION- How can I apply this to my life?**

Sunday John 6:59-71

Q:

A:

Digging DEEPER

Are you going to follow Jesus when things get rough? John points out two important truths in this passage. First, that Jesus knew from the *beginning*. This statement uses the same Greek word found in John 1:1 (the Word was with God in the *beginning*). This statement shows His foreknowledge, a characteristic that applies only to God. Secondly, verses 66 and 70 make it clear that just *following* Jesus does not guarantee that a person is a true believer. Many followers left Him. We will see later that Judas was a close follower but not a true believer in the Lord Jesus.

***Are you a true follower of the Lord Jesus Christ with a living and growing faith? Do one thing today to help your faith grow (study, memorize, or witness).***

Life stEP

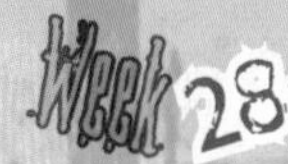

Monday John 7:1-13

Q:

A:

Digging DEEPER Do you think it would have been easier to believe in Jesus if we were alive when He walked on the earth? Most probably would not. We have something they did not have – God's Word. Many of Jesus' followers left because they weren't true believers. Today we see that His own brothers did not believe in Him yet. The climate in Jerusalem was unpredictable. The people did not know who to believe. The rulers of the Jews were seeking to kill Him. Still Jesus went up secretly to be part of the Feast of Tabernacles (a celebration where the Jews were reminded of God's provision while in the wilderness).

***Have you accepted God's provision of salvation? List the advantages we, as believers, have today and thank Jesus for them.*** Life stEP

Tuesday John 7:14-24

Q:

A:

Digging DEEPER Have you ever had a favorite teacher: one who could make the subject really come alive? Jesus was that kind of teacher. We see here that the people were amazed when they heard Him. He claimed His wisdom was from the Father above. God wants us to simply believe His Word by faith. Jesus tells of the miracle He did on the Sabbath – making a man whole. He compares it to the Law of Moses that allowed circumcision on the Sabbath. The Jews had changed their worship of God to following a set of legal rules to the letter, but God is always looking for obedience based on a relationship with Him.

***How is your relationship with the Master Teacher? What is the basis of your faith? Write it out and share it with someone.*** Life stEP

Digging DEEPER

Don't you love holidays? Families get together, and prepare special meals and activities that are only done during that time. The Feast of Tabernacles was about remembering and celebrating God's provision during 40 years in the wilderness after the Exodus. One important part of the feast was a procession of people from the Pool of Siloam to the Temple. Every day the High Priest led the procession carrying a silver pitcher of water that he'd pour out into the pool. With this backdrop Jesus proclaims that He was the source of true satisfaction and that those who find it would become a source of refreshment to others, referring to the work of the Holy Spirit that would come.

***Do you need refreshing? Come to the Source of Refreshment. Are you refreshing others?***

Life stEP

Thursday John 7:40-53

Did you know that your words reveal the attitude of your heart? They reveal what you are really like on the inside. The people in the early verses show their impulsiveness. They have a range of opinions about Jesus; some call Him the *Prophet*, others the *Christ*, and yet another group claims He couldn't be either. The Pharisees, on the other hand, blasted the people for their ignorance claiming that none of them believed in Him, like that was supposed to prove everything. All it proved was that in their hard hearts they lacked true knowledge about the Messiah. We see Nicodemus defending Jesus' right to a fair hearing before his peers and colleagues.

***What are your words telling others about the condition of your heart?***

Friday John 8:1-11

Q:

A:

Digging Deeper Have you ever been caught red-handed doing something wrong? This woman found herself in that situation. The Pharisees were trying to trap Jesus and discredit His teachings. They hoped to accuse Him of either contradicting Moses or breaking the Roman law (It didn't allow the Jews to inflict capital punishment.). Jesus knew what they were up to and avoided the trap by asking them a question that exposed their motives. Notice Jesus does not condone the woman's sin but releases her with the admonition to cease her life of immorality. She repented and was forgiven but was expected to forsake her sin.

*From what sin do you need to repent and forsake today? Ask God to show you an area on which you need to work.*

Life stEP

Saturday John 8:12-24

Q:

A:

Digging Deeper The Pharisees were intelligent, educated men, yet they argued intensely with the Lord thinking they could change Him with their reasoning. Surely they felt the power and meaning of His words when He said, "I Am the light…" Jesus was in the treasury of the Temple. Large lamps that were like hanging bonfires lighted it. Jesus made the comparison to the spiritual illumination He wanted to be in each human heart. Jesus' testimony was valid because He knew the answers to the big questions of life – *Who Am I? Where did I come from? Where am I going?*

*Do you know the answers to the big questions of life? Do you know the One who already knows the answers? Ask God to reveal a little to you.*

Week 29

**Who do you think you are? That question is asked in different forms this week as we continue to follow Jesus' life. Jesus continues to deal with the growing contempt of the Pharisees as well as the controversy that came after He healed a man who was born blind.**

*Prayer Focus for this week:*

**Q: The QUESTION - What is the writer saying?**

**A: The APPLICATION- How can I apply this to my life?**

Sunday John 8:25-36

Q:

A:

Digging DEEPER

Have you ever been frustrated telling a story because someone just didn't seem to understand what you were saying? That's a little of what Jesus is experiencing here. He is frustrated with the Pharisee's disrespect, and rightly so since He was clearly the Messiah with signs to verify His claims. Jesus also predicts His own death and gives specifics so that after it happened, the people would remember His prediction, know that He was telling the truth, and believe. In verses 31-32 Jesus revisits the two themes that John started the book with: the Word of God and the Truth.

***Who do you believe Jesus is? If He is your Messiah and Savior, share Him clearly with someone who needs to hear Good News today.***

Life stEP

Monday John 8:37-47

Q:

A:

Digging DEEPER Things were getting a little heated between Jesus and the Pharisees, especially when Jesus pointed out who their true father was. John uses the term *your father* three times. First, it's true: they were of Abraham's physical seed, but obviously not spiritual. Then, the Jews claimed God as their father, but Jesus tells them that if they loved the Father they would also love the Son, which they clearly didn't. Lastly, Jesus tells them they are sons of the devil, the father of lies, for they were doing his work. Jesus proved His claim of speaking truth on the premise that no one could charge Him with any sin.

***Who is your Father? What one thing can you do today to show (prove to) someone else who your Father is?***

Tuesday John 8:48-59

Q:

A:

Digging DEEPER Have you ever been so frustrated with someone that you asked, "Just who do you think you are?" Jesus tells these *sons of Abraham* that they didn't *know* by experience the heavenly Father like He inherently *knew* Him. We can almost feel the indignation from the crowd growing. Jesus understands where they are coming from but makes it clear He is not attempting to glorify Himself, but simply carrying out His Father's will. By the end of the debate, the people were ready to stone Him to death, especially after His clearest *I Am* (Jehovah) claim in verse 58!

***Who do you think you are? Plan how you will respond the next time someone challenges your claim of a relationship with the Lord Jesus.***

Week 29 Wednesday John 9:1-12

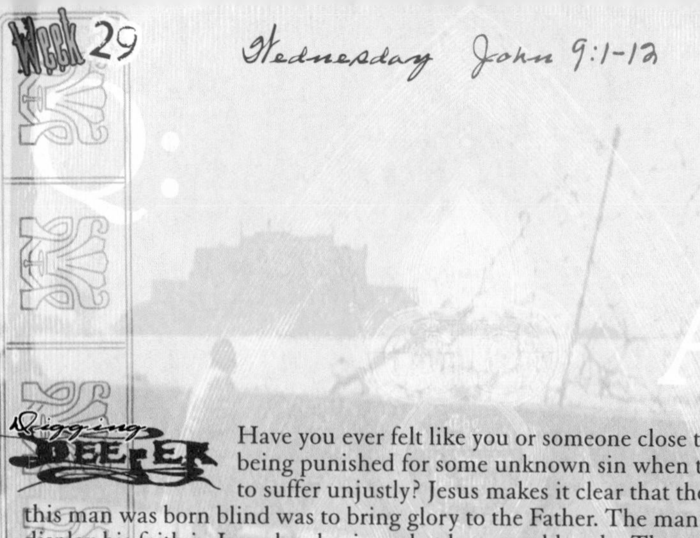

Digging DEEPER

Have you ever felt like you or someone close to you was being punished for some unknown sin when they seemed to suffer unjustly? Jesus makes it clear that the only reason this man was born blind was to bring glory to the Father. The man had to display his faith in Jesus by obeying what he was told to do. Throughout his Gospel, John highlighted specific miracles (signs) to show that Jesus is God and bring us to the point of believing in Him. Now He clearly illustrates this truth by bringing one born in both physical and spiritual darkness into the light.

***Does your life glorify the Father? Do you believe that Jesus is God? What is Jesus asking you to do to display your faith so others can see the light?***

Life stEP

Thursday John 9:13-25

Digging DEEPER

These verses show the tragedy of following man's tradition rather than walking with God. Clearly, a miracle had happened; no one was disputing that. However, the religious Jews were so spiritually blind that they could look right past an incredible miracle and only see a technical violation of their Sabbath tradition. It's interesting to watch the progression of the blind man's opinion of Jesus grow from the *man* (v. 11) to a *prophet* (v. 17) to *Lord, I believe* later in verse 38.

***What best describes your spiritual walk? Is it religion or relationship? Meditate on who Jesus is to you. Is He just a man, a prophet, or your Lord?***

Friday John 9:26-41

Q:

A:

**Digging DEEPER** Have you ever been around small kids and learned something profound from them? It is often the simple who instruct those who claim to be educated. The man clings to the truth that he was blind but now sees, and knows that it could only be by God's awesome power. He cannot help but believe in the One who gave him this great gift. The Jews called Jesus a *sinner* because they placed their Sabbath rules above the spirit of the law. When the man was *cast out* they kicked him out of the synagogue (the local assembly of the Jews). Jesus cares for, finds the man, and reveals His deity to him.

***What are you simply believing God for? Share with someone who is spiritually blind the One who can make him see.*** **Life stEP**

Saturday John 10:1-13

Q:

A:

**Digging DEEPER** "Just do what you believe in your heart and you'll get to heaven," or "If your good deeds outweigh your bad, you'll get into heaven." What is wrong with these statements? They are from the father of lies and are not true. Jesus makes His third and fourth *I Am* statements. First, He is the Gate. In those times, the shepherd literally lay down at night in the doorway of the stone corral to protect the sheep. The message is exclusive…*there is only one way*! (v. 7; John 14:6; 1 Timothy 2:5). Secondly, Jesus is the Good Shepherd. You've heard it all your life, but what does it really mean? To find out compare Zechariah 11:4-9, Psalm 22, Hebrews 13:20, Psalm 23, 1 Peter 5:4 and Psalm 24.

***Is Jesus your gate to heaven and your shepherd? Prove it by your actions!***

## Week 30

**Is Jesus your Good Shepherd? This would be a good week to decide. This week we'll see Jesus proclaiming His relationship with the Father which enrages the Pharisees who will seek to kill Him. We'll also see several situations where Jesus knows what is happening far away as well as in the future.**

*Prayer Focus for this week:*

**Q: The QUESTION - What is the writer saying?**

**A: The APPLICATION- How can I apply this to my life?**

*Sunday John 10:14-30*

Q:

A:

### Digging DEEPER

Is Jesus your Good Shepherd? John explains the special relationship that Jesus has with His sheep. It is the *knowing* that is important. The Father loves the Son because of His willingness to obey. Verses 17 and 18 clearly teach that Jesus was in total control throughout the events leading up to His crucifixion. He willingly laid down His life as a sacrifice for each one of us. This happened during the Feast of Dedication (today's Jewish celebration of Hanukkah in December). This passage concludes (vv. 27-30) with a powerful declaration of the security every believer can have in their eternal future.

***How secure are you in knowing Jesus as your Good Shepherd? Are you willing to obey anything the Father asks you to do? Think about it!***

Life stEP

Monday John 10:31-42

Q:

A:

**Digging DEEPER** Have you ever been upset by something someone else said? The Jews understood perfectly Jesus' statement in verse 30 that He and the Father are one. They lashed out calling it blasphemy. Jesus quoted Psalm 82:6 where the Psalmist used the common Hebrew word for God, *Elohim.* He also let His works speak for Him. Again, we see that Jesus was in complete control of the situation as He eluded their grasp when they wanted to stone Him. His ministry returns to where it began and many sought after and believed in Him there.

***Will you stand for God when challenged by the world? What do your works say to those around you about your relationship with Jesus?***

**Life stEP**

Tuesday John 11:1-15

Q:

A:

**Digging DEEPER** Do you know what goes on at you friend's house when you're at home, or what's going to happen tomorrow? Of course not! It's amazing to observe in this passage that Jesus, being God, not only knew what was going on at His friend's house (which was around 20 miles away!), but also what was going to happen four days ahead of time. He explained to His disciples that this episode was going to glorify both God the Father and Son. This final sign (miracle) before the crucifixion points to the newness of life that awaits those who have trusted Christ as Savior.

***Do you trust God to know about and be in control of what's going on in your life, both today and in the future? Write two things for which you are trusting Him.***

Wednesday John 11:16-29

To lose someone close to you is a very painful thing and everyone handles it in his own individual way. Martha ran to the Lord as soon as she heard He was coming and discussed the resurrection with Him. Mary waited and mourned until she was told that Jesus was near and wanted to see her. Here is something interesting to think about – the Jews of that day believed the soul of a person did not leave for heaven until three days had passed. Notice that Jesus purposely waited until the fourth day to increase the drama and impact of this crowning sign (miracle).

***Thank God for dealing with each of us as an individual. Ask Him to help you meet people where they are.***

Life stEP

Thursday John 11:30-44

Have you ever been surprised when something bigger and better happened than what you expected? Maybe it was for a birthday or Christmas. When Mary reached Jesus, she used words that were almost identical to the ones Martha had used. She showed a firm conviction that they believed Jesus could have saved Lazarus from death. Jesus exceeded all that they thought could have happened! Many Christians are like Lazarus when he came out of the tomb – alive in Christ, but still bound by the grave clothes of the world. They cannot work because their hands are bound, or witness because their mouths are also bound.

***If you are a Christian, are you totally free from the bondage of this world? Ask Jesus to reveal any area that binds you and ask Him to help you as you work on releasing it.***

Life stEP

Friday John 11:45-57

Q:

A:

Digging DEEPER What would you have done if you were in the crowd that witnessed Lazarus coming out of the tomb? Of course, you would believe, right? However, we see that some simply went to report the incident to the authorities. Their hearts were hardened to the truth. When the Pharisees discussed this new miracle, they openly plotted to kill Jesus (which Jesus predicted in John 8:44). The Passover was at hand. Jesus would soon be the ultimate Passover Lamb. His blood would be a once-for-all sacrifice that would serve not as a covering for sin (which Passover represented), but as the satisfaction of God's righteous demands (1 John 2:2). It was the cleansing from sin for those who believe (Hebrews 10:10-14).

*Share this story with someone and ask what he would have done?* Life stEP

Saturday John 12:1-11

Q:

A:

Digging DEEPER It is hard to distinguish time in the Bible. It would seem that the events in today's text happened shortly after Lazarus was raised from the dead, but they were about three months later. Martha was still serving while Mary was worshipping. The value of the perfume is overwhelming because it was rare, being from India. Would you give a year's wages for something then pour it on someone's feet? No one suspected Judas of thievery at the time. Mary, Martha, and Lazarus are wonderful examples of service, fellowship, and worship. Judas and the Pharisees are examples of greed and sinful intents of the heart.

***With which group do you line up? What are you willing to place at Jesus' feet?***

Week 31

Do you know what you believe about Jesus is the key to your future, and blessing is found in doing what pleases God? This week we'll see Jesus pleasing God from the time He entered Jerusalem with people who hoped He was the Messiah to quietly humbling Himself as He washed the disciples' feet.

Prayer Focus for this week:

**Q: The QUESTION - What is the writer saying?**
**A: The APPLICATION- How can I apply this to my life?**

Sunday John 12:12-22

Q:

A:

Digging DEEPER

Wouldn't you like to have been in the crowd that day? This is one of the few events recorded in all four Gospels so it must be significant. There is Old Testament symbolism here that an average person might miss. For example, the palm branch was a symbol of happiness. Hosanna means *please save*, while both this phrase and *He who comes* are found in Psalm 118:25-26. The crowd obviously had these messianic ideas in mind as they greeted Jesus. His entry, riding on a donkey's colt, is a fulfillment of Zechariah 9:9. Again, the disciples didn't fully understand what happened here until after the Resurrection.

***Read the above Scriptures to see how Jesus fulfilled them. All things written about Jesus will be fulfilled. Are you ready for His return?***

Life stEP

Monday John 12:23-36

Q:

A:

**Digging DEEPER** Did you notice that no more mention is made of the Gentile's request? However, Jesus uses this as an opportunity to predict His pending death. Verse 25 is a paradox. Those who wish to save their life (living for their own selfish ends) will destroy that to which they desperately cling. While those who hate their lives (by comparison) gain true life indeed. John returns to the familiar theme of light versus darkness and the faith that leads to belief.

***What are you doing with what you know about Jesus? Praise God for giving you the opportunity to enjoy special benefits as a child of God.***

**Life stEP**

Tuesday John 12:37-50

Q:

A:

**Digging DEEPER** Are you asking, "How could those who witnessed these miracles not believe"? It is hard for us, who have the whole Bible, to understand their hard hearts. Some who reject the deity of Christ say Scripture does not refer to Jesus by the name *Jehovah.* However, there is a direct connection in verse 41 that refers to Isaiah 6:1 where John tells us that the prophet beheld the glory of Jesus. Those who reject Jesus Christ only have themselves to blame. Jesus makes it clear that those who hear and reject the Gospel will be judged by the very Word of God from which they have turned away.

***How are you responding to the truth of the Gospel? Thank the person(s) who took the time to share it with you. Whom do you need to share it with?***

Digging Deeper: What would you think if the President of the United States came to dinner at your house and washed everyone's feet? Someone far more important washed the disciples' feet! Jesus showed His disciples how much He loved them by leaving them an example of humility to follow. In the exchange between Peter and Jesus, more than dirty feet was discussed. Jesus' reply in verse 10 is a reference to salvation. "He that is washed," (saved) needs only to wash his feet (confession of daily sins). Believers are bathed in the blood of Jesus Christ for salvation and kept in fellowship by the confession of daily sin.

***Who do you need to humble yourself before today? Let Jesus wash your feet (spiritually) by confessing your sin to Him.***

Thursday John 13:12-20

Did you know that washing feet was usually the task of the lowest servant of the house? Jesus explained that, as their Teacher and Lord, He was not too good to serve them. They were not too good to serve one another either. If our Lord was humble enough to wash the disciples' feet, who are we to consider ourselves above serving others, no matter how lowly the job? Blessing is not found in the knowledge of what is pleasing to God, but in *doing* those things that please Him. Jesus also plainly tells them of His betrayal before it occurred, so that after it happened, their faith would not be shaken but strengthened.

***Be like Christ and serve someone unexpectedly today? Do something that you know will please God (memory work, witnessing, or caring).***

Life stEP

Friday John 13:21-38

Q:

A:

**Digging DEEPER** Isn't it hard to be around someone you know is going to die? Jesus tells His disciples to brace themselves because He's going to be leaving them. They don't totally understand. Peter privately tells John to ask Jesus who the betrayer is. He asks and gets the correct answer when Jesus plainly identifies Judas. However, the other disciples were oblivious to what was going on. When Jesus tells them that they can't follow Him, He softens the statement by indicating that their separation would be temporary, not permanent. Jesus calls Peter on his intent to lay down his life for Him by stating the reality to come.

***Life stEP*** *Will you be able to follow Jesus like Peter in verse 36? Are you willing to lay down your life for Jesus? He knows the reality to come!*

Saturday John 14:1-14

Q:

A:

**Digging DEEPER** The sixth of Christ's great *I am* statements is found in verse 6. Jesus, being one with the Father, was of the same fundamental nature as the Father. To know Him was equal to knowing the Father. Belief is the key. Those who know Jesus know the way home! The astounding statement that the disciples would do *greater works* is understood as greater in scope. Jesus, who limited Himself by taking on an earthly body, was ministering in a specific geographical area. Now with the Holy Spirit living in believers, we have the privilege of seeing lives changed through the power of the Gospel all over the world at the same time.

*Do you believe Jesus and the Father are one? Act on it, and share who Jesus is with someone needing Good News today.*

Week 32

Have you ever been confused about the ministry of the Holy Spirit? Many ask, "Where does He fit in with God the Father and God the Son?" Jesus will reveal this week how the Holy Spirit convicts us of sin, encourages to righteousness, and helped the disciples write the New Testament.

Prayer Focus for this week:

**Q: The QUESTION - What is the writer saying?**

**A: The APPLICATION- How can I apply this to my life?**

Sunday John 14:15-24

Q:

A:

Digging DEEPER

Do you love God? You can prove it by obeying God's Word and Jesus' example. Verses 15 and 24 are like the bookends of this section. Obedience to the commandments of God characterizes the life of the true believer. Jesus set the ultimate example of love and obedience. Now He expects His followers to walk according to that same pattern. The *other* Comforter that Jesus used here is the Greek word *allos*, which means *another of the same kind*. Both Jesus and the Holy Spirit are of the same kind and should comfort us.

***Again, do you love God? Do the people around you see your obedience to God's commands? Think of one thing that you know God commands you to do in His Word and do it.***

Life stEP

Monday John 14:25-31

Q:

A:

Digging Deeper

Do you remember what your friends have said to you over the last three years? Jesus tells His disciples that one of the ministries of the Holy Spirit would be to help them remember all He had said, even when they didn't understand it at the time. The ministry of the Holy Spirit is different after the cross than before it. The actual payment for the sin of mankind gave the Spirit of God greater influence in the lives of men than Old Testament saints experienced. Notice that it was with unwavering obedience and submission to the will of the Heavenly Father that Jesus Christ walked full face into the adversary's fury.

Life stEP

***What is the Holy Spirit helping you remember from God's word? Is there something specific He's asking you to obey? Do it!***

Tuesday John 15:1-11

Q:

A:

Digging Deeper

As Jesus and the disciples left the Last Supper and went to the Garden of Gethsemane they passed olive gardens. Jesus used this as an analogy to describe the relationship He had with the believer. The result is increasing fruitfulness. The gardener prunes the branches that are in the vine to maximize their fruit bearing. Verse 7 is not a blank check but a promise that His disciples could rely on Christ to meet their needs as they walked in obedience. This relationship that Jesus describes for His disciples was based upon love and obedience, just as His relationship with His Father. Their walk of love and obedience would result in glory to the Father and fullness of joy for them.

Life stEP

***Are you walking in love and obedience? Are you being pruned?***

Wednesday John 15:12-27

In yesterday's passage, we see Jesus talking to the disciples about their relationship to Him. Today He talks to them about their relationship to each other. In that day, students chose the rabbi they wanted to study under. Jesus says He reversed the process by choosing them. He chose them to be fruit bearers. Jesus warns them that the world is not going to treat them kindly. The last two verses return to the coming of the Comforter who will energize them in their relationship. They will be as a light, a witness, and a testifier to the world. Notice that the Holy Spirit's job is to magnify Christ, not Himself.

***We are free to choose to show our gratitude to our Savior by working for Him and His glory. What can you do today to show your gratitude to Christ?***

Thursday John 16:1-11

Have you ever been confused about the role of the Holy Spirit? Jesus explains what's to come. There are three areas stated in verse 8 and explained in verses 9-11. First, the Spirit is to bring conviction of sin to the world. Second, the Spirit convicts of righteousness and sin among Jesus' followers. Third is the warning of coming judgment. Jesus warns them to expect to be cut off from the religious leaders so they were not caught off guard when it happened. Being put out of the synagogue was serious. Birth certificates, marriage certificates, divorce, and burial rights were all controlled by the synagogue and the Pharisees.

***Is the Holy Spirit convicting you of an area of righteousness that you need to work on? Judgment is coming! Are you ready?***

Life stEP

Friday John 16:12-22

Q:

A:

Digging Deeper Another part of the ministry of the Holy Spirit is teaching. Jesus pre-authenticates the whole of the New Testament writings to come. "Bring to remembrance" speaks of the Gospels. "Guide you into all truth" would occur as the Epistles were penned under the Holy Spirit's inspiration. These letters would give the early Church (and us) much needed direction and instruction. "Show you things to come" was the promise of the blessing of the completed Bible. The book of Revelation would foretell the final chapter of human history and the glorious future for those who enter into God's rest.

*What is the Spirit teaching you today? Let Him guide you in understanding God's revealed Word.* Life stEP

Saturday John 16:23-33

Q:

A:

Digging Deeper When was the last time you didn't pray "in Jesus' name"? Reference is made in verse 23 to a time after Jesus' Resurrection when the pattern to follow would be given. They were to pray to the Father in the authority of the Son and empowered by the Holy Spirit. It is hard to think that anything could be better than having Jesus living with you in the flesh. However, in the plan of God, the indwelling Holy Spirit and His written Word gives us a richer relationship with the Godhead. Jesus leaves an example for us to follow in our lonely times as He rightly pointed out that the Father would be with Him when He knew the disciples would flee.

*Consciously think about each person of the Godhead as you pray using the above pattern. Thank Jesus for what you know is going to come.*

Week 33

Have you ever dreaded an upcoming week? Perhaps you faced mid-terms or finals and you knew there was going to be a lot of stress? This week we'll see Jews trying to kill Jesus, Gentiles trying to free him, and others venting their frustrations on Him. With all this going on, Jesus stays focused on the job He came to do.

Prayer Focus for this week:

**Q: The QUESTION - What is the writer saying?**

**A: The APPLICATION- How can I apply this to my life?**

Sunday John 17:1-13

Q:

A:

Digging Deeper

Would you like the Lord Himself to pray specifically for you? He does here. This is Jesus' high-priestly prayer of intercession. Verses 1-5 is a prayer between Father and Son. Jesus asks the Father to "glorify Thy Son," meaning His authority, and to "glorify Thou Me," meaning His return to His pre-incarnate glory. Second, the prayer broadened to include the disciples. There are two commands in verses 6-19 to "keep them" (from evil) and "sanctify them" (set them apart for His work). Then verses 20-26 contain two requests, *I ask* for unity among all believers, and *I desire* to unite all believers with their Savior in glory.

***Are you part of all believers? Thank Him for praying for you! Are you living in unity with others and working together to do things that glorify Jesus?***

Life Step

Monday John 17:14-26

Q:

A:

**Digging DEEPER** Isn't it comforting to know that Jesus was looking down through history at us as He prayed? We are not of this world as shown in verse 8. First, we accept His Words. Second, we recognize that Jesus came from the Father. Third, we believe Him. Note the close association in verse 17 between sanctification (to be set apart for God's use) and revealed truth. Those 11 disciples began a long chain of unity and hard work that reaches down the corridors of time to us in the twenty-first century. Hopefully the result was your salvation! We are to take the disciples as our example. We are to be set apart and continue where they left off.

***Are you a promoter of unity, or are you a weak link by sowing discord in your local church? Thank those who shared Jesus with you!***

Tuesday John 18:1-14

Q:

A:

**Digging DEEPER** The Cedron (Kidron) was a steep valley between Jerusalem and the Mount of Olives. The band (cohort) of men that Judas brought numbered 300-600 soldiers! Christ responds with the name of Jehovah, "I Am." By the response of the soldiers, they knew what He said. This display of power is a reminder that Jesus did not have His life taken from Him but laid it down willingly. Peter tries to take charge of the situation. He does not realize that the events are part of God's plan. Jesus stops him and announces His intentions to go with the men. He is taken to Annas who was the real power behind the High Priest.

***Are you studying God's Word so that you might know truth from error? Are you fulfilling God's plan or trying to take charge yourself?***

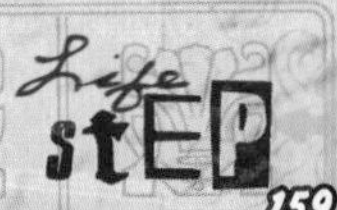

Wednesday John 18:15-27

Q:

A:

What would you have done as a witness to the events that night? Only two of the disciples followed Jesus at a distance; Peter and John (who doesn't record his name out of humility). The high priest's questions were directed at two areas: Jesus' disciples and His teaching. He was more concerned with who followed Jesus than what He taught. Interwoven among Jesus' questioning is the drama of Peter's denials. When comparing the four Gospel accounts, some have been confused about the identity of the questioners. Many people around the fire could have questioned Peter. Each author reported the questioner that caught his attention in the retelling of the events of that fateful night.

***What kind of witness are you? When under fire will you follow or leave?***

Thursday John 18:28-40

Q:

A:

Do your actions ever contradict what is going on in your heart? Look at how the Jews didn't want to go into the Praetorium (hall of judgment). They didn't want to *defile* themselves while they were in the process of planning a murder! Jesus answers Pilate clearly stating that He is a King, but not of this world. Note that Pilate does not probe the answer, but simply concludes that Jesus is indeed claiming to be a king. What he does next by asking "what is truth" seems to show an indifference to Jesus' words. Pilate appears to neither believe Him nor find Him to be a threat but looks for a way to set Him free.

***How are your actions portraying what is going on in your heart? Do those around you know of your belief in Jesus?***

Life stEP

Q:

A:

Have you gotten confused about the charges against Jesus? The original charge against Him before Pilate was treason (John 18:33).The Sanhedrin thought charging Him with treason would be easier than explaining the real charge of blasphemy. Pilate wasn't willing to execute an innocent man and beat Jesus to try to satisfy the Sanhedrin. Perhaps Pilate thought to arouse pity to release Jesus. He also allowed his soldiers to take their frustrations out on the Jews by mocking their *king*. Jesus maintains a dignified silence fulfilling Isaiah 53:7. Jesus minimizes Pilate's role in the Crucifixion by placing the blame on the Jews.

***These are not the best choices, but who would you select? The Jews who wanted Jesus killed, Pilate who tried to release Him, or the soldiers who took their frustrations out on an innocent man?***

Saturday John 19:12-22

Q:

A:

Digging DEEPER

Have you ever tried to trick someone into saying something? Pilate baits the Jews into professing heresy when they say, "We have no king but Caesar." From this, he realized the hardness of their hearts and turned Jesus over to be crucified. The purpose of Roman crucifixion was two-fold. First, the agony of the event was designed to discourage rebellion. The other was total humiliation. This was evident from the cruelty of carrying your own instrument of death to the shame of public nakedness. It is natural to concentrate on the physical horror of crucifixion but remember the spiritual results of the humiliation, selfless love, sin bearing, and the spiritual death.

***Think deeply about what Jesus did when He was willingly crucified for you.***

Week 34

This week is going to be exciting as we examine fulfilled prophecy, confusion about the Resurrection, and Jesus' appearances after the Crucifixion. John declares himself an eyewitness to all the things concerning Jesus' ministry. He wants the result of reading this book to be belief in Jesus. Do you believe?

Prayer Focus for this week:

**Q: The QUESTION - What is the writer saying?**

**A: The APPLICATION- How can I apply this to my life?**

Sunday John 19:23-30

Q:

A:

Digging DEEPER

Have you ever tried to write a mystery story where all the clues needed to be given, but in such a way that the solving was not obvious? It's a difficult thing. We see evidence of God's sovereignty in the fulfillment of prophecy (Psalm 22:18, 69:21) – even down to the number of soldiers involved. Jesus' concern for His mother is touching. *Woman* was not a disrespectful way to address one's mother in that culture. "Behold thy son" was instructive to Mary as He commends her to John's care (The care of a widow was the responsibility of the oldest son.). Jesus entrusts His mother to the care of John rather than His unbelieving brothers. Jesus' love and concern was evident to the end!

***Whom can you show love and concern for today in Jesus' name?***

Life stEP

Monday John 19:31-42

Q:

A:

Digging DEEPER Are you familiar enough with the Old Testament prophecies to know which were actually fulfilled in Jesus' first coming? Here John tells us of two more: Exodus 12:46 and Zechariah 12:10. This particular Sabbath was a *high* day. It was the first day of the Feast of Unleavened Bread that year. John injects some strong emotion (vv. 35-37) identifying himself as an eyewitness to Christ's death explaining what he saw. *Water* is the plasma that separates from the red blood cells after the heart stops. Two influential men secure the body, allowing it to suffer no more indignity.

***Look up the Old Testament passages listed the last few days and be a witness to someone of all that God fulfilled through Jesus.***

Life stEP

Tuesday John 20:1-10

Q:

A:

Digging DEEPER The ironic tragedy of the life of Jesus is resolved in the resurrection. "Although virtuous, He suffered all possible indignities; majestic, he died in disgrace; powerful, he expired in weakness. He claimed to possess the water of life but died thirsty; to be the light of the world, but died in darkness; to be the Good Shepherd, but died in the fangs of wolves; to be the Truth, but was executed as an imposter; to be Life itself, but He died quicker than the average crucifixion victim. The greatest example of righteousness the world had ever seen became a helpless victim of evil!" (Merrill Tenney)

***Think through the above statements carefully and thank Jesus for what He did for you. Share this with someone who needs hope today.***

Life stEP

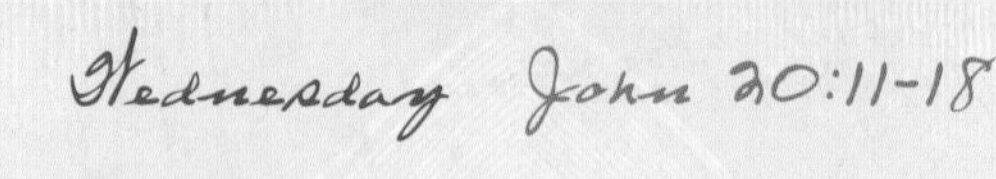

Q:

A:

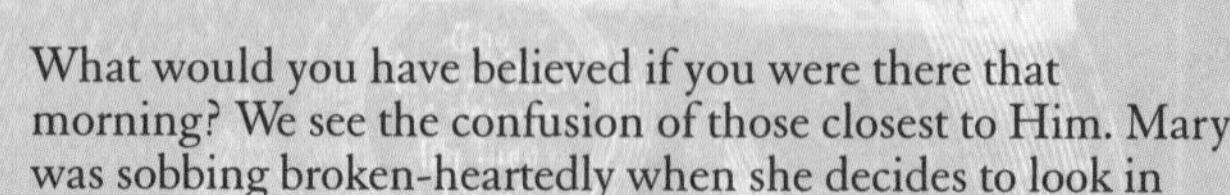

Digging DEEPER

What would you have believed if you were there that morning? We see the confusion of those closest to Him. Mary was sobbing broken-heartedly when she decides to look in the tomb. She sees the angels and talks to them but nothing is registering. She turns and notices another man and launches into a fresh attempt to locate the body of her Lord. Finally, through her tears, she hears the familiar voice and realizes she is talking to her Lord! Two natural acts follow. First, she uses the familiar name *Master* and then clings to Jesus with a grip that hinted she would never let go. Jesus didn't want Mary to cling to Him. She needed to go and tell others and then learn to trust Him by relying on the soon coming Holy Spirit.

Life stEP

***Mary was forgiven much and loved much. How much do you love Jesus?***

Q:

A:

Digging DEEPER

Wouldn't you like to have been one of the first to see the resurrected Lord? We don't know how many were gathered there that night. We do know they were afraid. Imagine how they must have been dissecting every detail that Mary, Peter, and John provided. Suddenly, Jesus was there. They were fearful of His sudden appearance and their actions earlier. Jesus spoke to them with a routine greeting of peace to calm their fears. Before we're too hard on Thomas, remember that the very proof he requested had already been provided for those who were there. The purpose of the book of John is clearly stated in verse 31, "… that we might have life through His name."

Life stEP

***Do you believe? Don't be afraid to share the Gospel with someone who doubts what the world has to offer. We know that Jesus is the answer!***

Friday John 21:1-14

Q:

A:

Digging Deeper

Having established belief in the life and message of Jesus Christ, John now tells us how this message spreads throughout the world. Jesus appeared to the disciples on their familiar home ground. This canceled out any sense that what they experienced in Jerusalem was a product of their fear and confusion. Christ appears to men who should have recognized Him, but they didn't. Jesus, being God, knew they hadn't caught any fish and tells them where to cast the net. They obey and realize it is the Lord as they remembered three years earlier when Jesus first called them to ministry.

Life Step

*Write down some things Jesus has done for you since you were saved. Thank Him for providing for you and share the Good News with someone.*

Saturday John 21:15-25

Q:

A:

Digging Deeper

Have you ever wanted to take back something that you said in frustration? Peter had publicly denied the Lord three times after professing a greater love than others. Now, Christ gives Peter three chances to affirm his love for Him publicly. The Master Shepherd mentions two aspects of shepherding – feeding and caring for all their needs. John closes his Gospel declaring that his life served as an eyewitness account of the greatest Man who ever lived. It was his desire for those who read his account to believe in the Lord Jesus Christ as their personal Savior.

*Do you believe? Are you willing to follow Jesus wherever He leads you and do what He asks? Would those around you affirm that you are a Christian?*

Week 35

Everyone needs wisdom and understanding to continue in better service for our Lord and the Word of God provides all we need. This week we are reminded that if we are going to have wisdom that comes from God we must start with a humble attitude and a willingness to learn from Him.

Prayer Focus for this week:

**Q: The QUESTION - What is the writer saying?**

**A: The APPLICATION- How can I apply this to my life?**

Sunday Proverbs 1:1-9

Q:

A:

Digging DEEPER

A driver rounded a sharp curve in the road only to find a road full of cows that had fallen from the back of a semi-truck. The truck overturned because the driver was going too fast and lost control. Most of the cattle died because the driver overestimated his skills and underestimated the curve. Knowledge is the accumulation of facts that helps us form conclusions. Wisdom is taking the principles that we learn (knowledge) and applying them to our lives. This is a key to living a Christian life. Just like the person who applies his knowledge of the road to drive safely, we are to study Scripture and then apply it to our lives. This is the way of wisdom.

***List one time that you failed to take good advice and twice when you did.***

Monday Proverbs 1:10-19

Q:

A:

**Digging DEEPER** In verse 10, Solomon instructs us to stand firm when sinners tempt us. In vv. 11-14, we see the way that sinners will entice. They will try to lure us in with promises of success. The reality of sin is that it does bring pleasure. If it was a sin to stick needles in our eyes, we would all be safe! We must remember that the pleasure of sin is only for a short time. A famous evangelist and his son noticed a billboard with a good looking man along side two pretty women hanging on each bicep as he held a beer in his hand. Underneath the billboard was a drunk sleeping off his stupor. The evangelist said "This is what the world tells you," and then pointing at the drunk, "and this is what the world gives you."

***List two reasons that we believe when the ungodly lie and entice us.*** **Life stEP**

Tuesday Proverbs 1:20-33

Q:

A:

**Digging DEEPER** Why do people hate knowledge? We see it every day when people reject the truth about the effects of drugs, alcohol, lack of sleep, or over eating. They won't listen to their doctor or anybody who offers sound advice. They are going to do whatever they want. Verse 22 reminds us that fools have hated knowledge throughout time. Verse 26 tells us that God's response to such foolishness is not to come to our aid when calamity or terror hits. We've all heard our parents say "I told you not to do that, now you have to live with the consequences" (vv. 28-32). Solomon says that there will be a time when they will reap the results of their evil life and they will finally want wisdom, but it will be too late.

***How would you go about helping a stubborn person see the truth?***

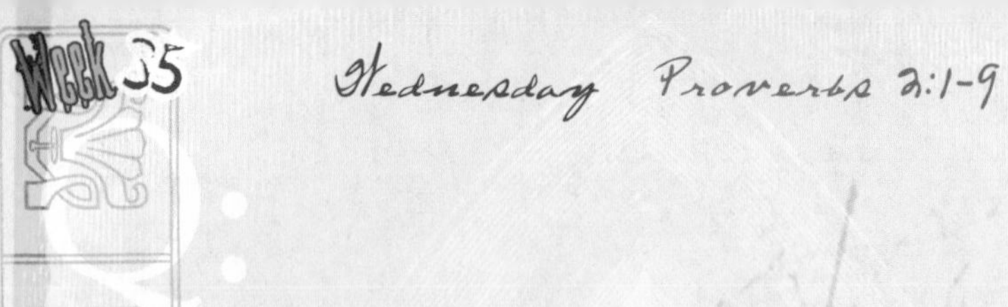

Wednesday Proverbs 2:1-9

Digging DEEPER What would you do if you were told that there was $1,000,000 worth of gold buried in your back yard? You would get busy digging to find it. The wisdom of the Lord is much more precious than all of the riches that the world has to offer. We should be willing to dig for it as we would dig for gold in the back yard. Verses 4-5 tell us that we will understand the fear of the Lord and find the knowledge of God if we seek it. This is the kind of seeking that parents do when their child is missing. They don't just casually look; they search with all their heart and strength. The Lord is calling for that type of heart attitude in this passage. He has wisdom stored up for us (v. 7); all we have to do is go to Him for it!

***List two things that hinder you in your search for wisdom. List two things that help you search for wisdom.*** Life stEP

Thursday Proverbs 2:10-22

"Good, better, and best. Never let it rest until the good is better and the better is best." Decisions based on the wisdom of God's Word are the best. Verse 11 reminds us that discretion, or good judgment, will preserve us. Good judgment comes from knowing and understanding God's Word. We make the wisest decisions in our lives when we make our decisions based on the long-term results of our actions as opposed to immediate gratification. The unwise make decisions to bring immediate gratification, and the result is disaster as Solomon observes in verses 18-22 when he considers the man who pursues an immoral woman.

***Write down the temptation you struggle with most. Write down the four best decisions you can make to help you avoid that temptation.*** Life stEP

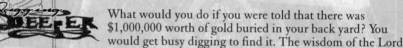

Friday Proverbs 3:1-8

Q:

A:

Digging DEEPER

"Trust me" is a common statement we all have used and heard others say. Trust doesn't come easily. It has to be earned. We don't trust just anyone to fly an airplane. We don't trust just anyone to do surgery; they must have the proper training and experience. Today's passage tells us to trust in the Lord with all our heart (v. 5). Solomon can say that with confidence because God doesn't make mistakes. He never sleeps. He never has to ask for help or advice. He has all the strength, power, wisdom, and knowledge to do whatever needs to be done. By contrast, we should not trust in our own understanding because we tend to rationalize away our sinful behavior that breaks our fellowship with God.

Life stEP

*The will of God for your life is that you trust Him. List four ways you can do that.*

Saturday Proverbs 3:9-18

Q:

A:

Digging DEEPER

When we invest our money in something, it is for the purpose of gaining more later on. People invest in land, gold, the stock market, even in other people with the intention of making a profit. When it comes to giving to the Lord, most of us take the money that rightfully belongs to God and use it on ourselves. We spend it instead of investing it. Verse 9 reminds us that all God asks of us is the first fruits or the first little bit we earn. He doesn't ask for all of it, just some, which is an indication of our love for Him. If we love God, we will give our time, effort, money, and our entire life. The blessing part is in verse 10. You cannot out give the Lord. When we give to Him, He blesses us beyond all we can imagine.

*Give a portion of your money to the Lord for two months and see the blessing.*

Week 30

No one likes to be called a fool or considered foolish. However, we all know someone who has made foolish choices and destroyed his life and testimony for the Lord. This week Solomon reminds us of the value of ruling our lives wisely and the result of foolish living.

Prayer Focus for this week:

**Q: The QUESTION - What is the writer saying?**

**A: The APPLICATION- How can I apply this to my life?**

Sunday Proverbs 3:19-26

Q:

A:

Digging DEEPER

We are told in verse 19 that it is by wisdom that God created the earth and all that is in it. To believe what the Bible says about creation, one must believe that there was one big miracle, and the rest makes total sense. God not only created the world, but he created it with great wisdom and care. The Creator has the right to rule over His creation. That is one of the reasons why people must believe evolution. If they believe evolution, they don't have to be accountable to the Creator. As opposed to evolutionists, our trust is in the Lord (v. 26), and we are willing to submit to His words of wisdom.

*Take time today to thank the Lord for all that He created and for your life. Thank Him for ruling over us with wisdom and care.*

Life stEP

Monday Proverbs 3:27-35

Q:

A:

Digging Deeper

It is uncommon for people to think of others before considering their own needs. When was the last time someone held the door open for you or went last in the line at a picnic or youth group feed? Our common thought is to try to be first rather than stop and serve others. In today's passage, there are five principles we should follow when dealing with people. First, we should do good to others whenever we have the opportunity. Second, we should give to others when we have the ability to do so. Third, do not think up evil against your neighbor, but be gracious. Fourth, we should not argue with others just to argue. It is one thing to make a case for the truth, but do it without arguing. Fifth, don't be jealous of those who oppose us.

*List three specific things you can do to be considerate. Then pray for help to do them.*

Life stEP

Tuesday Proverbs 4:1-9

Q:

A:

We know that all instruction in the Bible is excellent. Solomon tells us what he learned from his father, King David, when he was a child. God described David as *a man after my own heart*. He taught Solomon to guard the teaching he received and keep it in his heart. The *Word of Life* material emphasizes memorizing the Word of God as David did with his son. Many people have been taught that the key to life is to *live and learn*. That sounds good but it is not a biblical concept. The biblical principle is that we are to learn and then live. It is better to learn how to live in wisdom than to learn from mistakes! David taught this to Solomon. When Solomon could ask anything of the Lord, he asked for wisdom.

*Memorize Proverbs 4:7 and quote it to two other people.*

Week 36

Wednesday Proverbs 4:10-19

Everyone knows what it is like to walk a path in the dark, especially one that has holes, rocks, and limbs in the way. When we have a choice, we walk the path that is clear and easy. Solomon reminds us that we do have that choice in life and the wise person chooses to live his life so that his steps will not be hindered (v. 12). There is another benefit to walking wisely stated in vv. 14-19. The wise avoid the way of the wicked. We do not take their way of life, but observe the result of their sin and choose righteousness. "The path of the just *is* as the shining light… The way of the wicked *is* as darkness." (vv. 18-19) Which path have you chosen?

***List one area in which you need to change paths and walk according to God's Word instead of in the way of the wicked. Commit yourself to God and choose the path of righteousness.***

Life stEP

Thursday Proverbs 4:20-27

Did you ever observe a scene where someone is dying and he is trying to say something? Everyone bends down toward him and listens carefully to see if they can pick up what he is saying. That is the word picture in verse 20. We are to incline our ears to the way of wisdom and listen carefully to what it teaches. The Word of God brings perspective and life to all those who learn it (vv. 21-22). The emphasis in this passage is on what we let into our hearts. In verse 23, we are told that we are to guard our hearts. Soldiers are careful to guard the perimeter of their camp to make sure the enemy doesn't get in. Like the soldier, we are to set up a defense around our hearts to keep that which can harm us out.

***List two things you have allowed through the defenses that have harmed you.***

Friday Proverbs 5:1-14

Q:

A:

Digging DEEPER It is not news that we live in a sex-mad world. People have always been drawn by their lusts to immorality. The difference today is that media and the Internet bring the immoral images to us in an instant which makes these principles even timelier today. In verses 3-4, we are told that on the outside everything looks great and alluring, but the result of the activity is personal destruction. Sexual sin will eat away at your life unlike any other sin. Paul writes in 1 Corinthians 6:13-20 that there is something incredibly condemning about sexual sin. Our bodies belong to God for His use only. In verse 8 we are told not even to go near the house of an immoral woman. We should avoid all compromising situations.

Life stEP

*What sexual sins do you need to confess today? How will you avoid them?*

Saturday Proverbs 5:15-23

Q:

A:

Digging DEEPER God created our sexual desires. Within the boundaries of marriage, sex is a wonderful thing. Everything God creates is good, but Satan seeks to change it for evil. Drugs are a wonderful and useful thing for those who are sick. Satan uses those same drugs to produce addicts. This passage shows us that sexual activity is to be within the confines of a man and wife marriage relationship. One of the greatest gifts that you can give to your future spouse is a pure and holy life. Violating God's principles will carry implications in all of your future relationships, so it is vital to stay pure now. Surveys tell us that the average age that a young person loses their virginity is between 13 and 14. Christians are not to be average; we are to be excellent as we show Christ to the world.

*Ask God to keep you pure. Refuse to look or touch anything that God forbids.*

Week 37

Do you really think God is big enough to handle all your problems? It might be easy for you to answer "yes" when everything is going fine. But how about when things aren't going so well? This week we'll discover that God is big enough and far superior to anyone else, including angels.

Prayer Focus for this week:

**Q: The QUESTION - What is the writer saying?**

**A: The APPLICATION- How can I apply this to my life?**

Sunday Hebrews 1:1-7

Q:

A:

Digging DEEPER

Do you remember when you were a little kid and you brought something really cool to show your friends at school? You felt like the most popular kid in school until somebody else came in with something better. This is the idea the writer of Hebrews is sharing. They had the prophets' teachings revealing to them how God wanted them to live, but he shows how Jesus is so much better than the prophets are. Jesus is superior simply because He is the Creator of all things and He now sits with authority above all that He has created.

***How is Jesus described as being much superior to prophets and angels? Describe Jesus in a comparative way to great leaders, to politicians. List ways He is better.***

Life stEP

Monday Hebrews 1:8-14

Q:

A:

**Digging Deeper** Three are better than one! The Trinity is one of the most misunderstood doctrines in Scripture. When it comes to creation, the Father is represented by the architect; He planned it all. The Son executed the plans of the Father, as the contractor of the building. The Holy Spirit is represented by the various artisans who actually put the building together. When it comes to our salvation, the Father planned it in eternity past, the Son executed it at Calvary, and the Holy Spirit brought it to you at your conversion. This passage is explaining that God is so much superior to any of the other gods this original audience had encountered as well as any that we may come across today.

***What other gods do people worship instead of the one true God? How do we, as Christians, put other things above God crowding Him out of our life?*** **Life stEP**

Tuesday Hebrews 2:1-9

Q:

A:

**Digging Deeper** Have your parents ever explained something to you in agonizing detail? Maybe they wanted you to make sure you kept the stairway clear so your baby brother wouldn't trip and fall. However, you were too busy doing your own thing. Instead of listening, you ignored their instructions. In comes your brother at full speed, right into whatever it was you left on the floor. He trips on it and gets hurt. It is at that time your parents remind you of the power of the spoken word. It is the same in this passage. The author is reminding us to pay attention to our salvation so we won't drift away from it and fail to grow.

***Make a checklist of three things you should do daily to help you grow spiritually. How does God remind you of your forgetfulness to read His Word?***

Wednesday Hebrews 2:10-18

Q:

A:

You have probably known someone in school who was – well, a little bit different. Many times, there is someone who feels sorry for that person, talks to him, and does things with him. That someone goes out of his way just to make sure that "different" person doesn't feel left out or alone. He leaves the security of his own friends to make sure that everyone has a friend. Isn't that the way with Jesus? He's the Someone who left the treasures of heaven to come down to earth just so we could have a relationship with Him. We are just like that poor kid in school. Sin separated us from God, but Jesus reached out to us when we were most pitiful.

***How does God meet our needs? To whom is Jesus leading you to reach out?***

Life stEP

Thursday Hebrews 3:1-6

Q:

A:

We have all been around people who seem to do no wrong. They always get the teacher's praise, the awards, and are the pride of their parents. Everything they touch seems to turn to gold. God also blessed Moses for his obedience. Yet, even Moses needed to have faith in God. The author of Hebrews wants us to understand how ridiculous it is to compare ourselves with other people. The only One we should compare ourselves to is Jesus. Once we realize how far short we fall when compared to Christ, we will be less likely to compare ourselves to others.

***What are the characteristics that you admire most about your role models? What are some of the characteristics that you most admire about Jesus?***

Friday Hebrews 3:7-13

Q:

A:

"Clean your room!" Perhaps you have heard that command a million times. You have probably thought to yourself, "That just doesn't seem to make much sense. It will only get dirty again." What if we thought that about our walk with the Lord? This passage reminds us of the unfaithful Israelites who hardened their hearts toward the Lord. God blessed them by delivering them from the Egyptians, but they missed the blessings of the Promised Land!

*Have you ever disobeyed your parents, thinking that you had gotten away with it, only to find out that in disobeying you missed out on something they were going to do for you? Is there anything hidden in your heart that is keeping you from a closer relationship with the Lord?*

Life stEP

Saturday Hebrews 3:14-19

Q:

A:

Digging Deeper

Nathan raced for his birthday presents as soon as he walked in the door. Starting with the biggest ones, he tore through them at a frantic pace. Then he found the card that his grandparents gave him. He didn't even bother to open that. Later on the phone with Grandma, she asked if he liked his card, and he responded with a forced, "Oh, yeah." To which she replied that he should spend the $100 she placed in his card wisely! WOW, he had totally missed it! The stubborn Israelites were just like this selfish child at his birthday. God desires to give us so much more than we settle for. In our impatience, we take what we can get as long as we can have it *now*.

*Name one thing that you just had to have right away. Name one thing for which you had to save money. Which did you appreciate more?*

Week 38

Have you ever needed encouragement to start talking to your friends about Jesus? This week's verses are just what you have been waiting for! We do not have all the time in the world to tell our friends about Christ. We should tell them now, before it is too late.

Prayer Focus for this week:

**Q: The QUESTION - What is the writer saying?**

**A: The APPLICATION- How can I apply this to my life?**

Sunday Hebrews 4:1-11

Q:

A:

Digging DEEPER

What happened to the faith we had when we were first saved? It seems to fade as we live our life of faith. Many times, we begin to try to live our lives without God. God has more for us as we learn to depend on Him everyday. He promises that we will have rest for our souls if we trust in Him completely. This is where the Israelites failed. They quickly forgot the miracles God performed for them as He delivered them from bondage in Egypt. As a result, God led them into the wilderness.

***Why is it hard to depend on God's answer when you are experiencing trouble? Think of three ways that God has granted you rest by trusting in Him alone.***

Life stEP

Monday Hebrews 4:12-16

Q:

A:

Digging DEEPER Do you ever feel like no one truly understands what you are going through? You may talk to your friends or even your parents, but you can tell by looking in their eyes that they just don't get it. Sure, they listen intently, but they don't understand. You really do have Someone who understands. Talk with Jesus in prayer. He understands exactly what you are going through. When He walked the earth, He faced the same struggles you are facing and successfully overcame them. He promises to give you help in time of trouble and need.

***Think of something that is troubling you right now… something that you can't talk about to anyone. Talk to Jesus about it. Search the Scriptures and write down three things that Jesus struggled with but overcame.*** Life stEP

Tuesday Hebrews 5:1-8

Q:

A:

Digging DEEPER "You just don't know how good you have it." Have you ever heard that expression before? Sure, only about every time your parents have asked you to do something and you have responded to them with less enthusiasm than they expected. Seriously, we do have it pretty good when we compare ourselves to the people in the Old Testament. They had to rely on the priests to offer sacrifices for them. We can actually talk directly to God. Jesus was the perfect sacrifice, one that doesn't need to be repeated. Once we accept His sacrifice, we are made completely clean and can speak directly to God.

***Do you appreciate the privilege of speaking directly to God? Why not thank Him for it!***

Wednesday Hebrews 5:9-14

Q:

A:

They say that you can't tell a book by its cover. The same can be said of those who claim to be Christians. We can accept Christ as our Savior, go to church, have our quiet time, and say our prayers. But is our salvation affecting our lives? If we have truly accepted Christ as our Savior, there should be a dramatic change in our lives. Things should be different. With the Holy Spirit within us, as we study the Word of God, we should understand more of what He wants us to do. It will also reveal things that He does not want us to do. The problem may be resistance to the work of the Word rather than lack of the Word. We aren't going to be perfect once we accept Jesus, but we should at least desire to be.

***In what ways are your attitudes negative? Is God truly in control of your life?***

Thursday Hebrews 6:1-8

Q:

A:

"Grow up!" Not exactly words you enjoy hearing. God encourages us to press on to maturity in our walk with Him. He doesn't expect us to lie around and soak up the blessings of salvation and not grow in our relationship with Him. Once we are saved, He expects us to grow. We should be like a tomato plant firmly rooted in good fertilized, well-watered soil. We have no choice but to grow! If we fail to grow, God will cast us away like weeds in a summer garden. The more we resist God's voice in our lives, the less He will be able to use us. Our purpose is to come humbly before God with all that we have and allow Him to use us for His purpose.

***What are your spiritual gifts? How can you use them to honor the Lord?***

Q:

A:

**Digging DEEPER** Why do we fidget so much when we have to stand and wait in a long line? Why is it a struggle to wait until Friday to get our allowance? It is lack of patience. We've heard it a million times, "Be patient," or "Good things come to those who wait." Have you ever thought that patience is a sign of maturity – physically and spiritually? Think about a hungry little baby. He doesn't know how to wait. He wants his food immediately. We're not babies; we shouldn't be impatient with God. Our walk with Him should continue to grow and mature which includes many times when we will have to wait.

**Life stEP** ***The next time you have to wait in a check-out line, go to the longest one on purpose. Why do you think patience is so important to God?***

Saturday Hebrews 6:16-20

Q:

A:

**Digging DEEPER** *Hope* may unofficially hold second place only to *love* as being the most overused word in the English language. We *hope* it won't rain during the game. We *hope* that we get an "A" on our school project. With such a watered-down sense of hope, it is hard to see exactly what the writer of Hebrews is trying to share with us. In our everyday conversations, we hope for what we do not have. However, as Scripture explains to us here, if we place our hope in the living Christ, we have a living hope. Our hope is in the here and now. We possess what we are hoping in; that is, we have a relationship with Jesus.

***How is your hope in Jesus different than any other hope that you have? What do you think of when you think of hope?***

Week 39

Have you ever believed that the Old Testament was a waste of time to read or study? Hopefully this week's study of Scripture will change your mind. We are going to dig into some passages that show the importance of the Old Testament for us today.

Prayer Focus for this week:

**Q: The QUESTION - What is the writer saying?**

**A: The APPLICATION- How can I apply this to my life?**

Sunday Hebrews 7:1-10

Q:

A:

Digging DEEPER

Do you enjoy giving your things away? Is there anything that you hate more than having things around to enjoy? "Where am I coming from? What planet did I fall from?" you say. In these verses, we read about Abraham offering the Lord's servant a tithe. This offering helped the Lord's servant continue doing the Lord's work. God enjoys giving us things. One thing we need to remember is not to be selfish with the things He provides. It isn't a sin to have things, but God desires that we share them. We should be open-handed with our possessions – excited to share them with others. We should never be reluctant givers, but give with a glad heart (2 Corinthians 9:7).

*Name three things that you own that you feel you could never give up? Ask yourself why you couldn't. Are you putting too much importance on them?*

Life stEP

Monday Hebrews 7:11-17

Q:

A:

Digging Deeper

Have you ever thought of Jesus as a High Priest? What do you picture in your mind when you think of a High Priest? Maybe you think of the priests who were listening to the trumped up charges brought against our Lord before His Crucifixion. Is this who is meant here? No. The Old Testament law with its sacrificial system and priesthood could not save people. It could only give them a sense of how far they were from obeying it. A new system was necessary. Enter Jesus, our Great High Priest!

***Offer praise to the Lord, our High Priest, who has offered before the Father all that is necessary for us to have a relationship with Him. Can you think of anyone to introduce Him to today?***

Life Step

Tuesday Hebrews 7:18-22

Q:

A:

"Nothing in life is guaranteed, except taxes and death," so the saying goes. When we live following Jesus' perfect sacrifice, we can be assured that we will inherit eternal life. Heaven is sure for us because Jesus' death and resurrection secured what God required for salvation. Being born a sinner, we have nothing to offer a perfect, holy God that would allow Him to blot out our sins and transgressions. He paid it all! Think about that as you serve Him. Do not serve Him because of what you hope He will do for you, but what you can do for Him… with His help. It's not about us; it's all about God. With God, it is definitely who you know!

***Name three things that are impossible for you to do alone, but with God's help you can do them.***

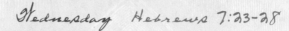

Wednesday Hebrews 7:23-28

Jesus, as High Priest, is altogether superior to the priests of the Old Testament. In fact, the Old Testament priests could only serve for a limited amount of time due the nagging inconvenience of death. Not so with Jesus! He lives forever to intercede, or go to the Father on our behalf. Even when we do not know what to pray for or how to pray for a particular need, Jesus stands next to the Father sharing our needs with Him (Hebrews 7:25). He has no motive except for our ultimate good. What an awesome God we serve!

***What makes Jesus' sacrifice better than those of the Old Testament? Why did the Old Testament priests continue to offer sacrifices over and over?***

Life stEP

Thursday Hebrews 8:1-6

Have you ever read through some parts of the Old Testament and wondered what the point is in reading that stuff? Some of the Old Testament seems unfamiliar when it talks about animal sacrifices, sprinkling blood on door frames, and waving grain in the air! These were all symbolic of what Christ would do for us as our great High Priest. Once you understand the sacrifice that Jesus made for us, you can better appreciate all the details of the sacrifices explained in the Old Testament. This is just one more reason we should stop what we are doing in our busy day and thank God for what He has given to us so freely.

***Name three duties of a High Priest. How are the promises offered by Jesus better than the ones offered in the Old Testament?***

Life stEP

Friday Hebrews 8:7-13

Q:

A:

Digging DEEPER Have you ever watched TV commercials that introduce a "new and improved" product? What are they trying to say? Was the old version worthless? No. They make these new claims so as to encourage us to purchase their new product. Similarly, as we read these verses in Hebrews, it would appear that the writer is telling us that this is what God is doing with the New Covenant. But that isn't what he is saying at all. The author of Hebrews wants to show us that, in the Old Testament, the Law shows us how far off track we are. The New Testament gives us hope by giving us a new heart. God gave us the very thing we needed in order to gain His favor – His Son.

***What is a covenant? How have you benefited from the New Covenant made by Jesus dying on the cross?*** Life stEP

Saturday Hebrews 9:1-10

Q:

A:

Digging DEEPER Have you ever gone to an amusement park with a friend? Perhaps you wanted to go on a ride together, but you were too short? No matter how you stretched your neck, you were still not tall enough. This reminds me of how it used to be in Old Testament times. God did not allow just anyone to come into the Temple and enter into His presence. The priest was only permitted to go in once a year. But, now all of that has changed. Jesus made all the difference. Now we can all enter into the Lord's presence through the finished work of Christ.

***Take time now to thank the Lord for letting you come to Him with every need that you have. What need is burdening your heart today? Share it with Him.*** Life stEP

Week 40

Have you ever read portions of the Old Testament and thought to yourself, "What is up with all of the animal sacrifices?" Hopefully, as we undertake our studies this week, that question will be answered. As you carefully read these verses, be attentive for words like sacrifice, cleansed, and forgiveness.

Prayer Focus for this week:

**Q: The QUESTION - What is the writer saying?**
**A: The APPLICATION- How can I apply this to my life?**

Sunday Hebrews 9:11-15

Q:

A:

Digging DEEPER

Completely – Totally – Once-for-all: these are words that describe what Christ's sacrifice did for us when it comes to the payment for our sin. The blood of imperfect animal sacrifices had to be offered by imperfect priests daily in order to satisfy God for man's sins. Jesus, the perfect High Priest, was the spotless sacrifice to satisfy the payment making it unnecessary for man to offer anything else. Our debt for all the sins that we have committed in the past, present, and even in the future, has been paid in full by the sacrifice of Jesus' death and resurrection.

*Why did Jesus only have to offer Himself once as a sacrifice while the Old Testament priest had to offer sacrifices more often? Can you think of a friend that needs to hear of this Good News?*

Life stEP

Monday Hebrews 9:16-22

Q:

A:

Digging DEEPER "If you get straight A's on your report card, you can choose any place you would like to go on your birthday," your Dad says. Wow! Wouldn't that be exciting! But, your excitement soon fades as you remember chemistry, physics, and history. As the year wears on, your grades are like a submarine, they drop below "C" level. You begin to get discouraged. What if someone offered to take your place and that someone could get A's in your classes? That's what Jesus did for us, not in chemistry, physics or history, but in real life. God demands perfection. We could never measure up. Jesus could and did! He became our substitute and because of His shed blood, we can find forgiveness in Him. We win!

*The New Covenant (Testament) was sealed by Christ's blood. What does that mean to you if you've trusted in Him as your Savior?*

Tuesday Hebrews 9:23-28

Q:

A:

Digging DEEPER Do you realize that when you placed your faith in Christ He delivered you from the penalty of sin (past), the power of sin (present), and that one day in the future He will even deliver you from the very presence of sin? Why is that? Because once you place your faith in Jesus, God identifies you with Jesus' death for sin and blesses you as He has blessed Jesus. Isn't that an awesome thought? You have been identified as a child of God. What a wonderful privilege! We can benefit from uninterrupted fellowship with God. The same way that Jesus talks to God, so can we!

*Christ kept our appointment with death for us and there is no more condemnation. Do you look forward to your daily appointment with Him in your quiet time for a time of communion?*

Life stEP

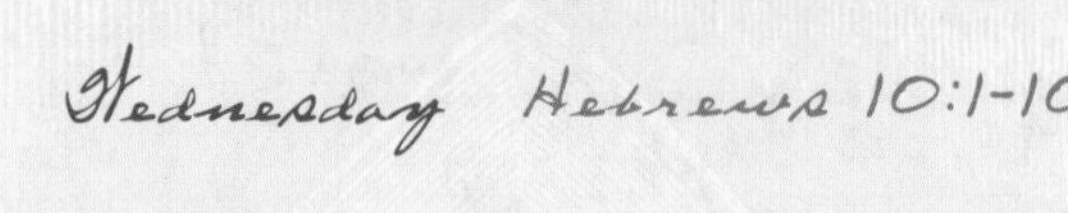

Wednesday Hebrews 10:1-10

Why all the sacrifices? In our passage today we see why those details were recorded for us. In Hebrews, the author shows us how Jesus was a perfect sacrifice and substitute. He only had to die once for all our sins since He had no sin. The Old Testament priests had to continually offer sacrifices because they were just as sinful as the people. All we need to do is trust in Jesus as our Savior and accept His gift of eternal life. God then accepts us into His family.

***Have you made that decision yet to trust Him as your Savior? If you are saved, list a couple of things you can do to show your love for the Lord or others.***

Life stEP

Thursday Hebrews 10:11-18

Have you ever had the pleasure of eating rotten meat? Mmmm! Let's add a whole bunch of salt, pepper, onions, garlic, and oregano? Would that take care of it? Yuk! Of course not! All of those extra ingredients would merely cover up the rotten meat. It wouldn't make it fresh again. It's kind of what our passage is saying here today. The Old Testament sacrifices never actually took away anyone's sins. That is why they had to be offered over and over again. There wasn't even a place for the High Priest to sit down because his work was never done. But Jesus' sacrifice of Himself was sufficient and only had to be offered once. Now He is seated at the right hand of God making intercession for us!

***Since our sins and iniquities will be remembered no more, why not offer a prayer of thanksgiving? Select someone to pray for that needs the Lord.***

Life stEP

Friday Hebrews 10:19-25

Q:

A:

Digging Deeper

Honestly, there may be many times when you question the real importance of going to church every week. I mean, after all, isn't it enough that you are saved, read your Bible, and pray everyday? Verse 25 of our Scripture reading for the day seems to answer our question. The Lord desires us to accept Him as our Savior, but He also wants us to spread the Good News as well. He knows our hearts. By coming together each week we can encourage one another, pray for one another, grow together, and join other believers in witnessing, praising, and worshipping Him together.

Life Step

***How important is regular church attendance to you? What other benefits can you gain from going to church regularly?***

Saturday Hebrews 10:26-31

Q:

A:

Digging Deeper

Appreciation. Respect. Thankfulness. These three words should come quickly to mind when someone does something for you that you did not earn or deserve. We should be especially mindful of all the Lord has done for us. We must continue to not take God for granted and remember to give Him thanksgiving for all He continues to do for us. If not, God will gradually remove His blessings to help us remember. If that doesn't work, He will eventually judge us for our thoughtlessness.

***List three things that God has accomplished in your life recently. List three ways you have shown your appreciation to the Lord lately.***

Week 40

Where does your hope lie? What is faith? In whom do you have faith? Faith in Jesus as your personal Lord and Savior is just the beginning of your journey in His family. God desires that we also use that faith in our daily walk with Him. We are learning to trust in Him, realizing that He knows best no matter what.

Prayer Focus for this week:

**Q: The QUESTION - What is the writer saying?**

**A: The APPLICATION- How can I apply this to my life?**

Sunday Hebrews 10:32-39

Q:

A:

Digging DEEPER

Do bad things ever happen to good people? What about to Christians? Of course they do. Since we know that God knows all things and that nothing happens without His permission, why does God allow bad things to happen? This passage helps us understand God's reasoning. When we endure hardships by trusting in God and obeying His will for our lives rather than giving up and trying to do things our own way, we will receive what God has promised.

***Can you think of an instance when you trusted God through a bad time? Can you think of someone who is going through a difficult time? Perhaps God wants you to witness about His faithfulness?***

Life stEP

Monday Hebrews 11:1-6

Q:

A:

Digging Deeper What is faith? We tend to throw that word around a lot. But, do we truly understand what it means to have faith in Jesus? Faith is knowing or understanding something to be true. We have faith in Jesus, not just because of the miracles He has performed, but because those deeds help us see that all He has said and done is true. But we must place our faith and trust in Him and trust Him with our future. After all, He's the One who knows the future and He is our trustworthy Guide.

***What can you do that will become a walk of faith? List two things you will trust God for this week.***

Life stEP

Tuesday Hebrews 11:7-12

Q:

A:

Digging Deeper Abel revealed his faith in his worship, Enoch showed his faith by his walk, and Noah demonstrated it through his work. Each was different but they all came as a result of a right relationship with the Lord. It's always encouraging to hear of those who have gone before us through hardships, yet remained faithful to the Lord. One thing about our faith which should strengthen and comfort us is the fact that no matter what happens to us as believers, we will never suffer God's wrath upon us. Since we have accepted Christ as our Savior, we are under the divine protection and shielding of the Lord.

***Which three do you best identify with: worship, walk, or work? Would others agree with your assessment of yourself?***

Week 11

Wednesday Hebrews 11:13-19

Q:

A:

Digging DEEPER

Is this as good as it gets? Thank the Lord, it is not. It is sad and depressing to see people put all their hope and dreams into efforts that won't last and invest in things with little or no eternal value. As believers, we must use our God-given faith to super-naturally "see" beyond this temporary home that we call earth and catch a glimpse of our eternal home in Heaven. It is there that we should place our hope. That is the sure foundation that can satisfy our deepest needs.

***Where are you placing your hope and trust? If it is in the Lord, it's a safe investment and one that is certain to pay rich dividends.***

Life stEP

Thursday Hebrews 11:20-29

Q:

A:

Another important characteristic of our new "eyes of faith" is that they help us to see beyond life's difficulties and trust the Lord's strength to help us in our time of need. Faith allows us to choose the difficult, yet right thing to do over the easy path. Although there may be many times we fail, God continues to be patient with us. Keep your "eyes of faith" fixed on Him and never turn to the left or right. We often suffer needlessly because we take our eyes off Him.

***It's always easier to keep our "eyes of faith" focused upon the Lord, than on self or man. List two things that you have trusted the Lord for in the last two weeks?***

Life stEP

Friday Hebrews 11:30-35

Q:

A:

One of the most awesome things about the Bible is that it includes stories of common people – people like you and me. It reveals not only their successes, but, more importantly, their failures. God didn't necessarily use gifted, talented or successful people to carry out His eternal plans. He chose people whom others may consider unworthy and useless to accomplish His life-changing plans and ministry. This further illustrates that He is in complete control. The events recorded here go far beyond mere human capabilities. Jesus said, "...greater works than these shall he do..." (John 14:12). We can expect some great things!

*How has God been able to use you lately? What were the results? What can you do to increase your effectiveness?*

Life stEP

Saturday Hebrews 11:36-40

Q:

A:

Digging DEEPER

All those listed in this passage went through great suffering to let their faith in God be known. Faith is the most powerful testimony one can share. Do you struggle to find just the right words to share when witnessing? Do you feel scared or inadequate? Is it hard to muster up the courage to begin a conversation about spiritual things? What is more important than sharing your personal testimony of faith? Whether you realize it or not, we *preach* a sermon everyday. We may not be behind a pulpit in church, but our actions, attitudes, reactions, and words all reflect the faith, or lack of faith that is in our hearts. We are a witness to a watching, critical, and unbelieving world.

*You are being watched. Pray for an opportunity to share your faith today.*

## Week 42

*What would Jesus do?* I know we have all heard that expression a million times, but it seems so important in our walk with the Lord. If we really want a deep, thriving relationship with Jesus, that question needs to run constantly through our minds.

Prayer Focus for this week:

**Q: The QUESTION - What is the writer saying?**

**A: The APPLICATION- How can I apply this to my life?**

Sunday Hebrews 12:1-8

Q:

A:

Digging DEEPER

Hard times are so much easier to endure when we have genuine friends cheering us on and encouraging us. We are often unaware of the power of sin. How easy it is for us to become distracted and fall. The author of Hebrews relates our Christian walk to a runner. To move swiftly and smoothly a successful runner must remove all that may get in his way. So it is with our walk with Christ. In order to grow more like Christ, we must avoid anything that hinders us or slows us down. He wants us to grow and go!

***List three things in your Christian life that slows down your growth process. Which one of these will you work on this week to help you grow faster?***

Monday Hebrews 12:9-15

Q:

A:

Who enjoys discipline? If we were disciplined more often, would we be happier? If you enjoy discipline, you're strange! However, let's distinguish between punishment and discipline. Punishment is correction when we have done something wrong. Discipline is used in order to teach us the importance of choosing what is best over settling for something less. Let's listen with an open heart to God's instructions as He teaches us to be more like Him. While discipline may not be fun, it helps us grow and become more like Jesus.

Life stEP

***What are some of the things that discipline teaches us? In what ways has God disciplined you? How has it changed the way you live your life of faith?***

Tuesday Hebrews 12:16-24

Q:

A:

Digging Deeper

We all make decisions every day. Some of them are important; others are not so important. Some decisions are between what is right and wrong. Then we must make decisions between what is good and what is best. The earth, which God created, is good. However, God did not create it to be worshiped, only as a clear testimony to Him. It should lead us to worship the One who created it. It is the same way when you see a beautiful house. You can stand and gaze upon its beauty. But when you meet the one who designed it, he is the one who is worthy of the praise for its splendor.

***Are you guilty of worshiping what God has given rather than God Himself? Your choices are important. Choose wisely today!***

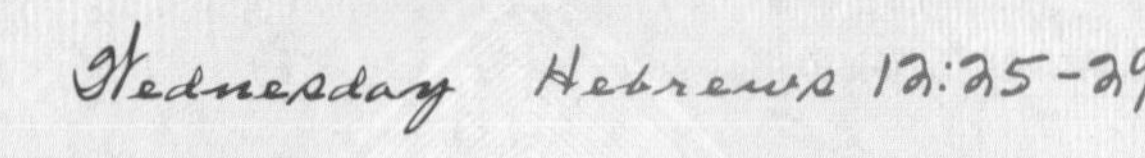

Digging Deeper

Have you ever received a really cool gift that included a really large instruction manual? After opening the package, you were so excited about your nice gift that you just tossed the instructions aside believing you could figure it all out for yourself. Then five hours later, you are sitting with an object in front of you that in no way resembles the picture on the front of the package. God has also given us a detailed set of instructions – the Bible. How does your life compare as you read it? Does your life resemble the One within its pages, or a *thing* created without reference to the instructions?

***How do you read the Bible, quickly or slowly? (Be honest.) How do you want God to listen to your deepest heartfelt prayers?***

Life stEP

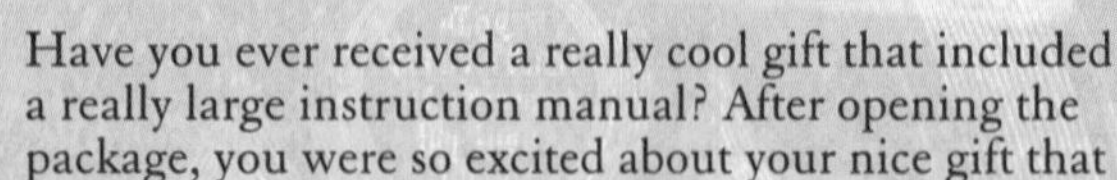

Materialism is all around us. Everywhere we look, someone is promoting something we just cannot live without. What should our attitude be toward possessions? We should be content with what we have. God knows what we need and promises to provide our needs (v. 5). Our world is preaching a very different message today. It tells us not to be content. We should look out for ourselves and do all we can to get to the top. No wonder the simple message of the Gospel proves to be a stumbling block to some, but the Word of God to others.

***Jesus can see all the things you buy with your money. Do you think He is pleased with your choices?***

Life stEP

Friday Hebrews 13:9-14

Q:

A:

Digging Deeper

A key thought that runs through other books of the Bible is "Do not be deceived by false teachings." With so many who teach false doctrines, it is important that we learn why we believe what we believe. We must be able to answer the questions that may arise from those who do not understand why we believe in Jesus and not in another religion. As we develop a good grasp of God's Word and understand what it says, we will be better equipped to ward off any flaming arrows before they strike us. It may also enable us to give an answer that will meet a need in their life.

*What are some false teachings that we hear today? How would you describe faith to a non-believer? If prompted by someone, could you give them a clear presentation of your personal testimony?*

Life stEP

Saturday Hebrews 13:15-25

Q:

A:

Digging Deeper

Do we still need to offer sacrifices to God in order to receive His forgiveness and blessing? Not in the same way as those in Old Testament times. The temple priests offered animal sacrifices. But in our passage today, the author tells us that we should offer sacrifices of praise to the Lord. This is done from a heart overflowing with thankfulness to God for all He has done and continues to do for us. Our heart should be overflowing with gratitude as we intentionally set aside time to think about all God has done for us.

***Choose a Psalm and personalize it to offer a sacrifice of praise to the Lord. What "good thing" (v. 16) can you do today that will bring honor and glory to the Lord?***

Life stEP

Week 43

What is the hardest thing you ever had to do? Jeremiah's name means, *Jehovah has appointed* and he lived up to his name by obeying the Lord in carrying out a very difficult work. This week we'll see the consequences God's chosen people had to endure because they didn't listen to Jeremiah and repent.

Prayer Focus for this week:

**Q: The QUESTION - What is the writer saying?**

**A: The APPLICATION- How can I apply this to my life?**

Sunday Lamentations 1:1-11

Q:

A:

Digging DEEPER

Have you ever lost someone close to you? There's a deep sense of loss and loneliness. Jeremiah describes the destruction of Jerusalem here using simple words indicating the prophet's struggle to express his grief. At one time Judah controlled Moab, Ammon and Edom, nations related to her through Lot and Esau. Now they treacherously join her enemy in attack. Jeremiah likens Jerusalem to an abandoned woman, referring to her as a widow and slave, being forsaken, captive, alone, and homeless. It is a fearful thing to fall into the hands of God in judgment. His holiness does not allow Him to overlook willful sin.

***Knowing that God didn't spare His chosen people from judgment, of what sin do you need to repent? Think about God's holiness throughout today.***

Life stEP

Monday Lamentations 1:12-22

Q:

A:

Digging Deeper Trouble and sorrow have a way of turning our attention back to a holy and just God. In this passage, the city of Jerusalem is speaking of the horror of her judgment and acknowledging that it was her own sin that brought on the judgment. She cries against her *friends* who not only didn't help her in her time of trouble, but even rejoiced in her sorrows. She asks God to judge them as He judged her. They will face judgment, too (Jeremiah 50-51).

***Are you facing trouble or sorrow right now? Don't presume upon God; let it direct your attention to Him where it belongs.***

Life stEP

Tuesday Lamentations 2:1-10

Q:

A:

Digging Deeper Do you know what your name means? In Biblical times the meaning of your name told a lot about who you were. In this passage, Israel means, *He strives with God*, and is referring to the time Jacob wrestled with God. It later became the name for the entire nation. Jacob is another designation for the nation, being the father of the twelve tribes. Judah was the *kingly tribe* and later became the name for the Southern Kingdom of Jeremiah's time. Notice that all three divisions of the Israelite government, prophet, priest, and king are all judged with the people.

***Study God's Word to learn from others' mistakes. God's people reap what they sow. What are you sowing? See Galatians 6:7.***

Life stEP

Wednesday Lamentations 2:11-22

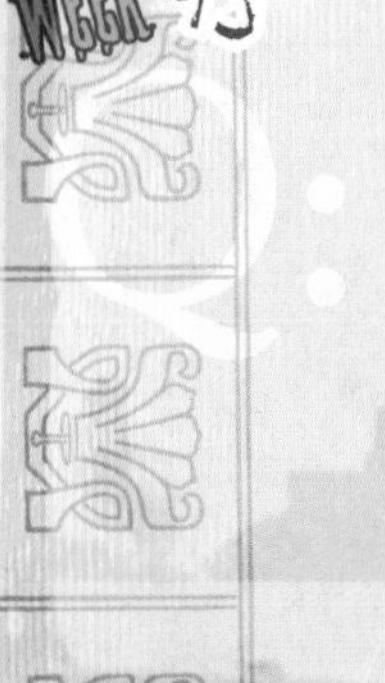

Digging DEEPER

When was the last time you grieved over something? Grief has a way of making us look inward. We first wonder what we may have done to cause it, then we look to God for understanding or a way out. Jeremiah speaks of his own grief in verse 11. Later he scolds the false prophets for not identifying sin as the cause of the impending doom. They even told the people that judgment would not fall on them. The people had no one to blame but themselves. God had forewarned that He would destroy any generation that disobeyed Him (Deuteronomy 28). Jeremiah asks the survivors to cry out to God with true repentance and receive God's forgiveness.

***Of what do you need to repent? Knowing and applying God's Word in your life will help you realize when others try to lead you astray.***

Life stEP

Thursday Lamentations 3:22-33

Digging DEEPER

Do your ever question what the Lord is doing in your life? It's a tendency we all share. Jeremiah does not question what God is doing, but he does express intense sorrow at the damage done to his country and fellow men. He then expresses confidence in the Lord. Jeremiah recommends patience in the face of suffering knowing that the Lord has His purposes. When His purposes are complete, He will return to His faithful ones with blessing. The one who complains during a trial is in danger of missing God's greater blessing. Knowing that God loves you and has a purpose for what you're going through should help.

***How are you responding to trials and hardship? Choose to praise the Lord and trust in what He has in the future.***

Life stEP

Q:

A:

Digging DEEPER When was the last time you had to give bad news to someone? It's not a fun thing, but that's what Jeremiah did faithfully for forty years. He preached that Judah deserved the punishment to come and counseled the people to accept the attack by Babylon. If they resisted, they would die. If they surrendered, they would live. In verses 40-51 he repeats the calamities that have befallen Jerusalem and challenges his fellow citizens to examine their lives. He relives the horrors of his own mistreatment at the hands of the kings of Judah in verses 52-57.

***What job has God given you to do? It may be to witness to a friend, memorize Scripture, or even do a difficult job. Do it faithfully like Jeremiah!*** Life stEP

Saturday Lamentations 5:7-22

Q:

A:

Digging DEEPER Is this passage teaching that these people were being punished instead of their *fathers*? No! These people were not totally *innocent*; they followed their *fathers* in sinning. In Ezekiel, talking about this same time period, God says He does not punish the children for the sins of the fathers, but that every man will be punished for his own sins (Ezekiel 18:1-9). As a result, these people were ruled by inferior men, risked their lives to find food, their bodies wasted away, their women were violated, their young men were forced into slavery, and even small children had to do hard labor. Jeremiah ends by calling for national repentance.

***Think about what these people had to endure. What do you need to do to avoid similar consequences? Jeremiah would suggest repenting!***

Week 44

When you think of 1 Corinthians you probably think of the love chapter. However, 1 Corinthians 13 is just one part of a letter from Paul to a messed up church. The Church in Corinth had many problems, and Paul's goal in this letter is to address as many of those problems as he possibly can.

Prayer Focus for this week:

**Q: The QUESTION - What is the writer saying?**

**A: The APPLICATION- How can I apply this to my life?**

Sunday 1 Corinthians 1:1-9

Q:

A:

Digging DEEPER

Aren't you glad that God is faithful? Even when we deliberately disobey Him, He doesn't give up on us. Even when we clearly rebel against Him, He doesn't abandon us. Even when we absolutely ignore His Word, He doesn't… ok, I'm sure you get the point. If not, the point is that even when we're at the point of giving up on God, forgetting our faith, or even dropping out of church, God remains absolutely faithful to us. Paul said it well when he said, "God is faithful." (v. 9). Our God really is a faithful God and He absolutely deserves our faithfulness in return. So let's give thanks to our faithful God and live our lives to honor Him.

***When was the last time you thanked God for His faithfulness? How faithful have you been lately?***

Life stEP

Monday 1 Corinthians 1:10-17

Q:

A:

Digging DEEPER Have you ever been a part of a church where no one seemed to be able to get along? If so, you're not alone. There are thousands of churches all over the world putting up with divisive people and their divisive issues. This is not a new problem. The Christians in Corinth had their own share of *divisions* (v. 10) much as many churches do today. While Paul doesn't go into all the details, this church obviously had a lot of arguing and fighting that had taken place and was still taking place. What the Corinthian Christians didn't realize, and what our churches today often fail to realize, is that God hates division in the church. On top of that, division brings shame to the name of Christ!

***Are you someone who usually causes division or brings about unity?***

Tuesday 1 Corinthians 1:18-31

Q:

A:

Digging DEEPER The Gospel seems so trivial, foolish, and unimportant to those outside the faith. They think it's foolish to believe that Jesus lived a sinless life, paid the penalty for our sins on a cross, and three days after dying, rose from the grave. However, to we who have experienced Christ's love and forgiveness personally, the Gospel is much more than some fanciful fairy tale. It is life and truth! It is far from unimportant. In fact, it is of utmost importance; so much so, that we cannot keep from sharing it with everyone we know because it is the best news ever!

***What makes the Gospel or "Good News" so good?***

## Wednesday 1 Corinthians 2:1-8

Q:

A:

Wouldn't it be great to have God speak through you? Wouldn't it be great to be used in this way? Paul experienced it firsthand during his ministry to the people of Corinth. As he stopped in Corinth on one of his missionary trips, Paul says that he didn't write a speech, design a talk, or prepare a sermon for this occasion. No, in fact, he says that God's Spirit gave him the exact words he needed to say and that he wasn't about to ruin that with his own words, thoughts, or ideas. Like Paul, it would be good for us to let God's Holy Spirit have His way with our lives and mouths in whatever situation we may find ourselves.

***What do you think it would be like to have God speak through you? What do you think it would take for that to happen?***

Life stEP

## Thursday 1 Corinthians 2:9-16

Q:

A:

What does it mean to have the mind of Christ? It's very obvious that we have the mind of Christ (v. 16), but what exactly is it? To have the mind of Christ means to think like He thought. When we have the mind of Christ, we'll begin to think about lost people the same way Jesus did. When we have the mind of Christ, we'll begin to think more about loving our parents, loving our friends, and even loving our enemies. When we have the mind of Christ, we'll speak the words of Christ, live the life of Christ, and share the love of Christ! In summary, to have the mind of Christ is to be like Christ in our character, words, and actions.

***Do you have the mind of Christ? How would your life be different if you did?***

Life stEP

## Friday 1 Corinthians 3:1-8

Q:

A:

**Digging DEEPER** Taking care of a baby is hard work! It seems like you are constantly feeding him a bottle, soothing him during a crying episode, or worst of all, changing him due to a…well, you know. It's hard work, right? As a result, it can be potentially frustrating. Now, imagine an adult who acts like a baby. He needs to be fed every two hours, takes four naps a day, and won't be quiet unless you stick a pacifier in his mouth. Now that would be a problem, wouldn't it? More than that, it would be really weird! Nevertheless, this is what Paul sees in the church of Corinth – Christians who haven't grown up! Paul addresses these immature believers as babies who need to put their pacifiers down, take their bibs off, drop their bottles, and start growing up as Christians.

**Life stEP**

***In what ways and areas do you need to grow up as a Christian?***

## Saturday 1 Corinthians 3:9-15

Q:

A:

**Digging DEEPER** What are you doing that will last forever? While much of your life may be dominated by text messaging, trips to the mall, and telephone conversations, what are you doing that really matters? The reason why this question is so important is that one day you will stand before our great and holy God and He will do a rigorous and thorough inspection of your life. Only what's done for His name's sake will ultimately last and matter. This makes the earlier question so important, so here it is again – what are you doing that really matters?

***How much time do you waste on an average day? What could you do today that would make a difference in eternity?***

Week 15

Sometimes it helps to have someone talk to you plainly about mistakes you've made or sins you've committed. Paul continues his letter by addressing specific sins that seem to trap the Corinthian Christians. Pay close attention as these sins are still prevalent in the church, if not in your own life as well.

Prayer Focus for this week:

**Q: The QUESTION - What is the writer saying?**

**A: The APPLICATION- How can I apply this to my life?**

Sunday 1 Corinthians 3:16-23

Q:

A:

Digging DEEPER

God lives in you. How cool is that? Think about it for just a minute. The Holy Spirit Himself lives in you! When we fully let this truth sink into our life, what kind of difference will that make? It will certainly affect the places we go and the people with whom we hang out. It will probably affect the relationship we have with our parents to some extent. It will most likely change how frequently we open God's Word and spend time listening and talking to Him. The truth is it should affect every aspect of our life! God really does live in you and it might be helpful for you to just write down *God lives in me* on a 3x5 card and put it somewhere where you'll see it and be reminded of it often.

*Can your friends and family tell that God lives in you?*

Monday 1 Corinthians 4:1-13

Q:

A:

**Digging Deeper** Have you ever used the phrase *God knows my heart*? We normally use this phrase when someone has accused us of wrongdoing or suggested that we've been deceitful in some area. We use the phrase defensively to let them know that whether they believe us or not, God knows the attitude behind everything that we just said or did. While we may not realize it on a daily basis, God really does know our hearts. He knows our secret thoughts and sees our shameful behavior. We don't stand a chance of hiding from Him. One day, according to verse 5, He'll bring our deepest and darkest moments to light and expose us for what we really are.

***How's your heart? Are you ready to stand before God?***

Life stEP

Tuesday 1 Corinthians 4:14-21

Q:

A:

**Digging Deeper** We appreciate truth tellers. We're thankful for the people in our life who give it to us straight. While we may not always appreciate that rebuke or that correction when it happens, we always end up appreciating it later. Truth tellers are valuable and everybody needs at least one of them in his life. Paul was a truth teller and while he writes the Corinthians in love, there's plenty of power to his words. In fact, as this letter unfolds, Paul speaks as plainly as any writer of Scripture does, addressing such topics as immorality, lawsuits, and marriage among other things. He doesn't back down as he confronts the Corinthian Christians directly concerning their sin, but instead he gives it to them straight.

***Do you have any truth tellers in your life who will give it to you straight?***

## Wednesday 1 Corinthians 5:1-13

Q:

A:

**Digging DEEPER**

Are you hanging around Christians who are regularly disobeying God? If so, get away from them as quickly as you can. You must avoid them at all cost! Now, we're not saying that you avoid non-Christians who don't know any better. We mean, how can we possibly reach the lost if we don't know anybody who is lost? To some extent, we must hang around people who don't know Christ. The problem comes when we associate with Christians who know better, but choose to rebel against God. Paul says that the Christians who live like the world are the ones we need to avoid.

***Who do you need to stay away from until he begins to follow Christ again as he should?***

**Life stEP**

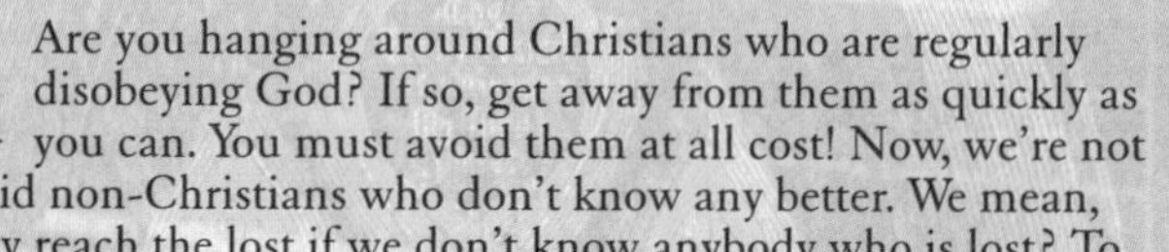

## Thursday 1 Corinthians 6:1-11

Q:

A:

**Digging DEEPER**

We need to be known as the kind of people who are passed our past. As Paul gives us a list of dangerous sins, he adds these words, "and such were some of you" (v. 11). The key word in that sentence is, obviously, were. It's not such are some of you, but such were some of you. So what made the difference? Well, we could use the doctrinal words, *justification* or *sanctification* to describe what took place in their lives. But the bottom line is that Jesus made the difference! He still makes all the difference in the world today. He can take the worst situation imaginable in our lives today and one day say to us "such were some of you" about the great change he brought about in our lives.

***How has God changed your life up to this point? How are you different?***

Friday 1 Corinthians 6:12-20

Q:

A:

**Digging DEEPER** There are some verses in the Bible that just make us go, "Wow!" 1 Corinthians 6:19 is one of those verses. When we read that the Holy Spirit lives inside us it just blows our mind! Think about this for a minute. The very God who created the universe and everything in it also lives in you in the person of the Holy Spirit. It's certainly a little difficult to swallow, but we come to the conclusion that, nonetheless, it's true. God lives in us. Because He does, we have a responsibility to live our life as if He were with us at all times, because the fact of the matter is, He is!

*What difference does it make that God lives in you?*

**Life stEP**

Saturday 1 Corinthians 7:1-9

Q:

A:

**Digging DEEPER** Marriage is a good thing. Actually, it's more that that – it's a God thing. God instituted marriage way back in the Garden of Eden. He even said, "It is not good that the man should be alone" (Gen. 2:18). Paul obviously agrees with God, and adds that if a man loves a woman, "it is better to marry than to burn" with passion for her (v. 9). Paul is directly confronting yet another problem in the church at Corinth, specifically, sexual immorality. Paul's solution was a simple one – get married and really be committed to each other. This command is equally applicable today. The church needs husbands and wives who will take their marriages seriously and be committed to one another for life.

*Why does God have such strict guidelines when it comes to marriage?*

Week 48

When God speaks, we must listen. We must never get to the place where we ignore His promptings and quit reading His Word. God wants to speak to us just as He wanted to speak to the Corinthians, and we must be open to the same truths and principles that He revealed to them.

Prayer Focus for this week:

**Q: The QUESTION - What is the writer saying?**

**A: The APPLICATION- How can I apply this to my life?**

Sunday 1 Corinthians 7:10-24

Q:

A:

Digging DEEPER

Marriage is for life! Divorce should not be the norm in the Christian's life. Unfortunately, we live in a world where divorce is unbelievably rampant and even accepted as normal. Perhaps the saddest part is that the Christians in our churches seem to be just as prone to divorce as men and women outside the church. God made marriage for keeps, and to have couples divorcing over pets, chores, and finances is ridiculous. God made marriage for keeps and we must understand that it's *'til death do us part.*

***Why do you think God hates to see a divorce take place? Why is it so important to stay married?***

Monday 1 Corinthians 7:25-40

Q:

A:

**Digging Deeper** One advantage that a Christian has in remaining single for his whole life is that he can be *sold out* to God. He can serve and minister in ways that a married man would find impossible. Obviously, the single person's concern would not be for his spouse or his kids as in the case of a married man. Therefore, his focus as a single person could be on pleasing God and God alone. His life can be a life lived for the glory of God. Now let me be perfectly clear – this doesn't make marriage a bad thing. It just means that being single doesn't have to be a bad thing, and in fact, has the potential to be an awesome thing.

***Have you ever considered being single as a possibility for your future? Are you willing to pray about that?***

Tuesday 1 Corinthians 8:1-13

Q:

A:

**Digging Deeper** Although we who are Christians have much freedom and liberty in our lives, we must be very careful not to live in such a way as to cause a younger, newer Christian to turn back to his old habits and hang-ups. Even though we may engage in an activity with a clear conscience, and with no sin in our hearts, we could hurt a Christian who is new to the faith by our behavior. We must be careful to be above reproach in our daily lives. While we ourselves can walk in absolute liberty, we must be continually aware that others could be hurt by our actions and choices.

***Are you willing to give up your freedom to do something that would negatively affect another Christian?***

Life stEP

## Wednesday 1 Corinthians 9:1-10

"Am I not free" (v. 1)? What a great question! Perhaps we should think about using this question periodically in our own lives. The next time someone says, "Why are you wearing sandals in December?" we can just reply, "Are we not free?" Of course, Paul wasn't talking about that kind of freedom necessarily, but he was saying that even though he was an apostle and missionary with his own share of responsibility, he had freedom in Christ just like everyone else. He wasn't bound to some man-made set of rules. The same is true for us! We don't have to be enslaved by a bunch of rules that aren't for us. We're free – free to obey Christ.

***What does it mean for a Christian to be free? Are you free?***

Life stEP

## Thursday 1 Corinthians 9:11-18

Your pastor deserves a paycheck! The Apostle Paul spells it out very clearly that it's not wrong for a pastor, missionary, or evangelist to get paid for what they do to help the church. In fact, it's not only acceptable, it's strongly encouraged. Although Paul himself didn't accept any money for doing what he was doing as a missionary to Corinth, he says that it's more than appropriate to pay those who lead the church. While you may think your pastor doesn't do anything but sit around the church and study, nothing could be further from the truth. So again, pay your pastor, but more than that, love him and pray for him.

***Do you appreciate all that your pastor does? When was the last time you told him thanks, sent him a card of appreciation, or prayed for him?***

Life stEP

Q:

A:

Digging DEEPER

Are you willing to do whatever it takes to see the people in your life accept God's forgiveness and surrender their lives to Christ? Paul said that he was willing to do anything that didn't violate Scripture to reach someone with the Gospel. He said, "I am made all things to all men, that I may by all means save some" (v. 22). Briefly, Paul's idea of reaching people focused on meeting men and women right where they were. He didn't say, "My way or the highway!" when it came to ministry. He adapted to his audience. We could learn a lot from his example as we strive to share Christ with those we know. It involves self-denial and self-control.

*Are you willing to do whatever it takes to see people in your life accept God's forgiveness and surrender their lives to Christ?*

Life stEP

Saturday 1 Corinthians 10:1-11

Q:

A:

Digging DEEPER

No grumbling allowed! I think that would be a good announcement for us to make from time to time in our churches on Sunday. For whatever reason, the church can become a place of grumbling and complaining. Now, grumbling is *not* a good thing. In fact, just say the word *grumble* aloud three or four times and you'll see that it even sounds bad. Among many other prohibitions Paul mentions as he writes to the Corinthian Christians, he also adds, "No grumbling allowed!" The actual word Paul uses is *murmur*, but it means the same thing as grumbling or complaining. The bottom line is that murmuring, complaining, and grumbling have no place in the church or in your life!

*Are you someone who complains a lot? What could you do instead?*

## Week 47

Satan hates the church! He will use whatever he can to disrupt, divide, and destroy it. Therefore, the church must be awake and aware, not giving in to the various temptations that come to us as individuals or the church as a whole.

*Prayer Focus for this week:*

**Q: The QUESTION - What is the writer saying?**

**A: The APPLICATION- How can I apply this to my life?**

*Sunday 1 Corinthians 10:12-22*

Q:

A:

**Digging DEEPER**

Temptation is tough! Some would be *tempted* to say that temptation is easy to ignore, but that's just not true. Some would be tempted to say that they've never been tempted, but that would be an outright lie. Temptation, when it happens (and it happens very often), is tough to deal with. For instance, we're *tempted* to put down our pencil right now, write a note or play a game, and just neglect our quiet time, because everything within us says we deserve a break today. However, we must not listen to temptation. As soothing as its voice is, in the end, it brings nothing but pain and misery.

***How do you deal with temptation? Do you give in? Do you trust God to help you?***

Life stEP

Monday 1 Corinthians 10:23-33

Q:

A:

Digging Deeper

1 Corinthians 10:31 is one of the first verses we are encouraged to memorize because it will help us establish priorities in our lives. "Whether therefore ye eat or drink or whatsoever ye do, do all to the glory of God." What a great verse! This means that when you're eating, it's possible to eat for God's glory. This means that when you go fishing, it's possible for you to do it for God's glory. This means that when you're reading, playing an instrument, competing in sports, or going for a jog, you can do these activities for God's glory. We could go on and on and on, but you get the point. Whatever you do, be sure that you are doing it for God's glory and not your own or anyone else's.

*What do you need to start doing for God's glory?*

Tuesday 1 Corinthians 11:1-10

Q:

A:

Look at me! This is Paul's advice to those who just aren't sure how to live the Christian life on their own. In continuing his instructions to the Corinthian churches, Paul says, *Follow me*, *Watch me*, or *Imitate me*. That's what he means when he says, "Be ye followers of me, even as I also am of Christ" (v. 1). He says this, not because he thinks he's the best role model ever (although he is a great role model), but because he is following, watching, and imitating Christ Himself.

*Who are the men and women of God that you look up to? What have you learned from them about following Christ?*

Wednesday 1 Corinthians 11:11-22

Q:

A:

Why can't we all just get along? Have you ever been in church and asked yourself that question? Unity is a word that should describe the churches where we worship. However, disunity is often the word that most accurately describes many of our churches. Think about this for a minute. If we all love Jesus, and we all worship the one and only God, and if we're all desiring to live by the Holy Spirit's power, what's the problem? The problem is that we often don't love Jesus enough, we worship ourselves quite frequently, and we don't depend on the Holy Spirit to guide us in the Christian life. So let's do something different for a change. Let's get along!

***How can you contribute to a spirit of unity in your church?***

Thursday 1 Corinthians 11:23-34

Q:

A:

The Lord's Supper is not a joke! Yes, we drink out of little cups and eat tiny, little crackers, but we must understand that the Lord's Supper is not about food – it's about Jesus! The church of Corinth evidently had problems taking this seriously, and there are many still today who don't treat the Lord's Supper with the reverence it demands. Let's just briefly summarize the Lord's Supper for anyone who may be unfamiliar with it. It is a special time when Christians gather to remember Jesus' sacrifice by eating bread (which represents His body) and drinking juice (which represents His blood). In doing this, we are obeying Jesus' commandment to remember what He did for us on the cross.

***How seriously do you think you should view the Lord's Supper?***

Friday 1 Corinthians 12:1-11

Q:

A:

Digging DEEPER You are gifted! Really, you are. The Bible says you've been given a gift by the Holy Spirit. You have been given a spiritual gift. Now, ask yourself a question: Do you know what your gift is? Besides our passage today, there are several other lists given in the New Testament (Romans 12; Ephesians 4; 1 Peter 4) that tell us about spiritual gifts. If you're a follower of Christ, you've been given at least one spiritual gift. You need to stop being *ignorant* (v. 1), and find out what your gift is and begin to use it to help others.

***Do you know what your spiritual gift is? How can you use it to help others and glorify God?***

Life stEP

Saturday 1 Corinthians 12:12-20

Q:

A:

Digging DEEPER You are a part of the body of Christ and you have a role to play within the body. You may only be a knuckle or knee, but you're still a part of the body and have a role to play within the body. You may not be the brain, heart, or mouth, but you are still a part of the body and have a role to play within the body. You may only be a small, almost invisible, seemingly unimportant part, but you're still a part of the body and have a role to play within the body. Let me repeat it again, you are part of the body of Christ and you have a role to play within the body! So what are you waiting for? Do your part!

***What role can you play in your church? Are you currently playing that part or are you just sitting around?***

## Week 18

The church has been described in all sorts of ways throughout the years, but perhaps the best description of the church is found in 1 Corinthians. The church is a body. It functions best when every part is working with every other part, and is a total failure when one part tries to do it all.

Prayer Focus for this week:

**Q: The QUESTION - What is the writer saying?**

**A: The APPLICATION- How can I apply this to my life?**

Sunday 1 Corinthians 12:21-31

Q:

A:

Digging DEEPER Aren't you thankful for a digestive system that functions properly, a set of lungs that helps you breathe, and a heart that beats to keep you alive? Even though no one can see your large intestines, lungs, or heart, the truth is they're more important than your eyes, ears, teeth, and hair. If it wasn't for those hidden body parts, you would die. In the body of Christ, there are certainly those members who aren't very prominent as well, and yet they are so important in making sure the body functions properly. Now as to what part of the body you might be, we're not sure, but you have an obligation to function to your maximum potential. Now, go and do it!

***What can you do to help your church grow and be healthy?***

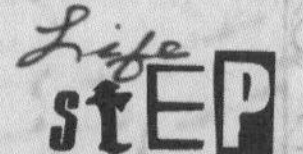

Monday 1 Corinthians 13:1-13

Q:

A:

**Digging Deeper** Love is so important. Without it, it doesn't really matter what you say, how much you know, how much money you give away, or how unselfish you are. While we're talking about how important love is, let's remind ourselves not to water down this word like we're so tempted to do. Let's stop saying, "I love pizza" or "I love basketball," and in the very next breath, talk about how much we love our parents, church, or Savior. Since love is so important, let's get it right. In fact, let's read this passage over and over and over again, all through our lives, until the message finally sinks in, and we really learn to love.

*After reading this passage, how loving would you say that you are?*

**Life stEP**

Tuesday 1 Corinthians 14:1-9

Q:

A:

**Digging Deeper** One of the ways the early church was able to grow so fast was through the spiritual gift of *tongues*. On several occasions throughout the Scriptures (see Acts 2 for an example), we see God's Word communicated by ordinary men to people of other nationalities and languages. Miraculously, God spoke through these ordinary men in a foreign language so that their audience would understand and be able to respond to the Gospel. However, as the church settled in different regions of the world, Paul asked this important question in verse 6, "…if I come unto you speaking with tongues, what shall I profit you…?" It's a good question to ask and one we must continue to ask today. Whatever is spoken should be understood by all who are there.

*What if your pastor preached in French this Sunday? Would that be useful?*

Wednesday 1 Corinthians 14:10-17

Digging DEEPER

When someone repeats something to you, what are they trying to do? They are attempting to make sure you fully understand what they're saying. If they continue to repeat something over and over again, they want you to fully understand it to such an extent that you will never forget it. This is what Paul seems to be doing as he continues to talk about the subject of the spiritual gift of *tongues*. He wants them to understand the purpose of this gift is not for worship services where it only causes confusion. In fact, he summarizes by saying, "…I had rather speak five words with my understanding…than ten thousand in an unknown tongue" (v. 19).

***In what areas of your life does God continually seem to repeat Himself?***

Life stEP

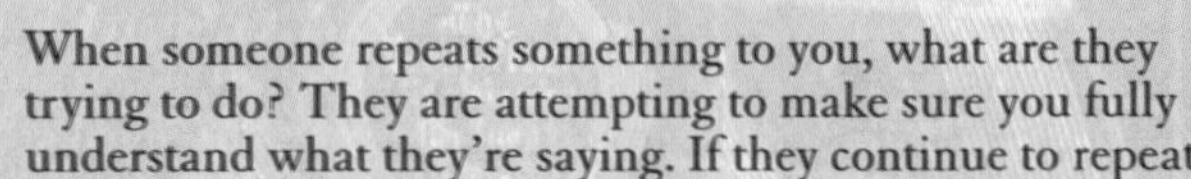

Thursday 1 Corinthians 14:18-26

Digging DEEPER

It's time for you to grow up! Seriously, in some ways, it's time for you to stop being so childish. The Corinthian Christians struggled to understand so many spiritual issues because they just weren't very spiritual. Unfortunately, since the time of the Corinthian Christians, the followers of Christ haven't progressed much. We're still as immature as many of the Corinthian Christians. It's time that we grow up! If you've been a Christian for more than a couple of years now, you should be in the process of growing up in the faith. As Paul puts it, "be not children in understanding" (v. 20). So take off your bib and start reading your Bible. Get out of the high chair and start memorizing some Scripture. Grow up!

***Are you becoming more or less like Jesus every day?***

Q:

A:

Digging DEEPER God knows what He's doing. He's never confused about what His role is or what He's supposed to be doing. Paul even says, "God is not the author of confusion" (v. 33). While we may be confused, perplexed, or puzzled about various issues in the Scriptures, we can rest assured that it's not God's fault. In fact, the truth is, we've created much of the confusion in our churches ourselves. Not only that, when we're not creating confusion, Satan himself does all he can to wreak havoc and create confusion. While our churches may not face the same situations the Church of Corinth faced, you can be sure that the enemy will do his best to bring confusion in our churches today.

*What kind of confusion does Satan bring into churches? How about your church?* Life stEP

Saturday 1 Corinthians 15:1-11

Q:

A:

Digging DEEPER It's not Easter, but let's say it anyway – Jesus is alive! Isn't that the best news you could hear today and the greatest truth of all time? In fact, just put down your pencil and say, "Jesus is alive" aloud a couple of times. Now some people find it hard to believe that Jesus is alive. However, to have over 500 eyewitnesses on your side makes a strong case. Not only that, most of those 500 eyewitnesses died for their belief that Jesus wasn't dead, but indeed alive! So, while it's not Easter, I'm still excited. Why? Because Jesus is alive!

*Since you haven't seen Him, why do you believe Jesus is alive today?*

Week 49

No letter lasts forever. While Paul certainly had much more he could have said to the Corinthian Christians, he chooses to wrap up his letter with some encouraging news about our future life with Christ.

Prayer Focus for this week:

**Q: The QUESTION - What is the writer saying?**
**A: The APPLICATION- How can I apply this to my life?**

Sunday 1 Corinthians 15:12-19

Q:

A:

Digging DEEPER

If Jesus didn't rise from the dead, then Christianity has a major problem! In fact, if Jesus didn't rise from the dead, then Christianity is pointless, Sundays are pointless, sermons are pointless, and life itself is pointless. Perhaps you've never thought of the Resurrection as that important, but it's as important as any other belief, and more important than most! If Jesus didn't rise from the dead, then our sins have not been forgiven, our faith is foolish, and our eternal destiny is certainly not Heaven.

***How important is the resurrection? If Jesus wasn't alive, what would that mean for you?***

Monday 1 Corinthians 15:20-28

Q:

A:

Everybody dies. Now that's kind of a morbid way to begin a paragraph, but it's true. We're all going to die. Everybody we know is going to die. Obviously this is very bad news. However, there's some good news. In fact, it's better than good – it's great! Because of what Jesus did for us, we don't stay dead. The truth is, when we close our eyes for the last time in this life, we open our eyes to a life beyond our wildest imagination; a life with God that will never end.

***Aren't you thankful that when you die, you don't stay dead? What would it be like to live without that kind of hope?***

Life stEP

Tuesday 1 Corinthians 15:29-38

Q:

A:

Digging DEEPER

Wake up, come to your senses, and stop living a life of sin! This is the message Paul gives to those in the Church of Corinth who just don't get it. In fact, he goes on to say, "I speak this to your shame" (v. 34). He questions whether they even have a relationship with God. This message is equally relevant today as people everywhere claim the name of Christ but live in a way that contradicts what He modeled and taught. How can we be so dumb? Let's get out of bed, wipe the sleep out of our eyes, turn our backs on the dead-end path of sin, and follow Christ with everything we've got!

***With what specific sins do you struggle? Why haven't you given it up yet? Are you ready to wake up?***

## Wednesday 1 Corinthians 15:39-50

Q:

A:

Have you ever wanted a new body? Maybe you wanted a muscle-bound body, much like a body-builder. Maybe you wanted a model's body that's perfectly proportioned, or an athletic body, much like your favorite baseball, basketball, or football player. Maybe you're pleased with the body God gave you (as you should be). If you've ever thought about having a different body, you'll be glad to know that one day you will receive a new body and it won't be similar to anything you've ever seen before. It will be a body that never ages, decays, or becomes weary or sick. It will never wear out. More than that, Paul says that our bodies will *bear the image of the heavenly* (v. 49). In other words, we will have an eternal body. Can you say, "Wow?"

Life stEP

***What do you think it will be like to never age or get sick again?***

## Thursday 1 Corinthians 15:51-58

Q:

A:

Digging DEEPER

Death and sin are powerful. They are two forces no one except Christ has been able to avoid and overcome. However, one day they will be completely abolished and we will be able to say with Paul, "O death, where is thy sting? O grave, where is thy victory" (v. 55)? When Jesus comes back to take His Church with Him, death is defeated and sin is beaten. They are both irrelevant at that point. Certainly this is a reason to celebrate and give thanks to God who put an end to sin and death by sending His Son, Jesus, to destroy it.

***How great will it be for you to finally be removed from the power, penalty, and presence of sin?***

Life stEP

Friday 1 Corinthians 16:1-12

Q:

A:

**Digging DEEPER** Are you a giver? It's very likely that you don't make a lot of money at this stage in your life, but when you actually do bring home some *bacon*; will you hoard it all for yourself or give some of it away? As followers of Christ, we should be known as people who give. In fact, Paul says that those of us who follow Christ should give a certain part of what we've been blessed with back to the Lord. Rather than establishing giving as a habit in your adult years, why not start this habit today? You'll never be able to out give the Lord.

***What can you give to the Lord this week?***

Life stEP

Saturday 1 Corinthians 16:13-24

Q:

A:

**Digging DEEPER** Whenever we finish writing a letter, we always conclude with some sort of friendly ending. We want the recipient to know that everything we've written comes from someone who loves and cares about them. Paul, as he finishes up his comments, leaves his readers with several encouraging sentences. He says, "The grace of our Lord Jesus Christ be with you" (v. 23), and then follows that up with, "My love be with you all in Christ Jesus" (v. 24). Although his words have been rough at times, Paul wants his friends in Corinth to know that everything he wrote comes from someone who loves them and wants God's best for their lives.

***Who can you encourage today with your words?***

Week 50

*Dead Man Talking* Paul is about to be executed for his faith. He has one last book to write and send to one person. One of the godliest men who ever lived writes his last words of advice. This is the real deal! This is hard core Christianity. Give this study your best! You won't regret it!

Prayer Focus for this week:

**Q: The QUESTION - What is the writer saying?**

**A: The APPLICATION- How can I apply this to my life?**

Sunday 2 Timothy 1:1-7

Q:

A:

Digging DEEPER

Paul is writing a very personal letter. He is about to die, and there is one last thing he wants to say to his close friend who will keep the ministry going. The last time they were together, they probably parted in tears. That's the last picture Paul has of Timothy. We learn that Timothy was often fearful and timid. Without Paul around, I'm sure Timothy felt like he didn't want to go on – but that's just the opposite of what the Lord empowered him to do. Any *fear* we have about living for God doesn't come from Him. If we trust and obey Him, He can make us incredibly powerful – able to do anything – absolutely anything…even if we feel timid!

***What does God want you to do that you are afraid to do? How has God gifted you? Are you using what God has given you for His glory?***

Life stEP

Monday 2 Timothy 1:8-12

Q:

A:

**Digging Deeper** Wouldn't it be great if we were living in heaven right now? No problems, no sin, no worries, a perfect body, *no fear.* Be honest – don't we all have things that cause us to fear? What if you could actually enjoy some benefits of heaven now before you're actually there? You can! Paul was faced with death for following Christ, something we probably haven't had to deal with. Paul knew that death was just a short little bridge to heaven with his Savior. If God didn't want him to die – He wouldn't. If he did – he'd be in heaven. So what is there to fear? God has called us to live a holy life. We need to give Him our best. Enjoy heaven today!

***Do you live out your security in Christ? What should you do to show others you are not ashamed of being a Christian?***

Tuesday 2 Timothy 1:13-18

Q:

A:

Heroes and Zeroes – that is who we read about today. We are introduced to three people. Only one of them was not ashamed of Christ or being connected to Paul. When the rumor got out that Paul was in prison in Rome, Onesiphorus did whatever it took to find him and be an encouragement. We need to realize our responsibility to minister to fellow believers. We should not ignore them when they need our help and support. "What! I'd never do that!" Jesus said, "…as ye have done it unto one of the least of my brethren, ye have done it unto me." A day will come when we will need the support of fellow believers. We will reap what we sow.

***Do you work hard at supporting fellow believers? Do you know a Christian who often is persecuted (or made fun of) that you could encourage today.***

Wednesday 2 Timothy 2:1-7

A:

"Impossible!" Some of us like the sound of that word because we want to try to do anything that someone says is *impossible*. Others aren't interested in being tricked into trying something they think is too hard. Either way – God is in the business of doing the impossible. The secret is in verse 1 – *Strong in grace*! By ourselves, we aren't very strong – but believing God's grace can empower us to do the impossible …now that's *strong*! That's how to become a *strong* Christian. Part of being strong is never giving up. Verses 3-6 give three illustrations of people that have to work hard and not give up. By God's gracious empowering – you can do anything He wants you to do!

***What challenge is there in your Christian walk that seems impossible at the moment? Will you ask God to help you learn about being strong in grace?***

Thursday 2 Timothy 2:8-14

A:

Have you ever missed the chance to witness to someone? You had the opportunity to share about Jesus, and you blew it. Me, too! That's part of our aim as Christians. Paul, the writer of 2 Timothy, was great at using every opportunity to witness. That's what led to his suffering in prison. However, it was time for Timothy to step up to the plate and be a witness like Paul. Timothy probably missed opportunities, also. That's why verse 13 is so awesome! God's Word can never be held back or chained up. The great news is that God wants to use you! Unfortunately, missionaries and pastors die like everyone else. Who is going to take their place? Who is going to reach your friends now?

***Who should you be praying for to receive Christ? Would you focus on sharing Christ with at least one person in the next three days?***

Life stEP

Friday 2 Timothy 2:15-19

Q:

A:

Digging DEEPER Did you know the Bible is the most read book in all of history and around the world today? Amazing? What's even more amazing is the number of people who disagree on what it actually says. That was the problem in today's passage. Verse 15 tells us there's a right way to handle it. Verses 16-18 are examples of people who didn't handle God's Word correctly. Yes, God's Word can be hard to understand, but you'll never regret studying this book! It's not a school book! It's God's Word! If you desire it enough, He will help you understand it.

***Do you ever skip over passages you don't understand? Would you be willing to ask people that can help you? How important is His Word to you?*** Life stEP

Saturday 2 Timothy 2:20-26

Q:

A:

Digging DEEPER You've got to cut through a four inch board. You have two choices. You can use a brand new stainless steel power saw or a flimsy plastic knife. I know the choice is easy. But some Christians are about as sharp as a plastic knife for God's glory. We're not a pure clean tool just like verse 20 describes. We're not useful and ready to be used. Verse 22 gives you the plan for staying clean. *Run! Flee! Stay away* from anything that keeps you from being a person God can use for His glory. Perhaps we have Christian friends who aren't so sharp for the Lord. Verses 24-26 show us how to help them. Note the words *kind* and *gentle*.

***What sin do you need to run away from? On a scale of 1-10, how sharp and ready are you for God? Is there another Christian you can help sharpen?***

Week 51

We learn what Paul was thinking as his life came to an end. But in truth we learn how to live it each day! Wait until you reach chapter four. It's almost a little sad. Paul is so brave and focused on Christ; nothing could shake his faith! He wants you to really know the Word of God by: Studying it through, Praying it in, Living it out, and Passing it on!

Prayer Focus for this week:

**Q: The QUESTION - What is the writer saying?**

**A: The APPLICATION- How can I apply this to my life?**

Sunday 2 Timothy 3:1-7

Q:

A:

Digging DEEPER

What a list! At the top, is the one that describes all the rest – *lovers of their own selves.* Please take note of verse 5! Some of these characteristics might be things we struggle with, but as a Christian, we should be changing and growing – always striving to be more like Christ. Perhaps you know of someone described in verses 5 and 7. He may call himself a Christian, but he doesn't have a life to back it up. He pretends to be godly and learning, but certainly isn't. We need to stay away from that person. The question isn't, "Is he a Christian?" rather, "Is he a *growing* Christian?"

*Do any of these characteristics describe you? What are you going to do to change? Who are the Christian friends you should hang out with the most?*

Life stEP

Monday 2 Timothy 3:8-12

Q:

A:

Digging Deeper

Who wants to live a godly life? (Hopefully, you answered "*me.*") Now, who wants to be persecuted? Most of us probably wouldn't sign up for that one. Verse 12 makes it clear that the two go hand in hand. Remember this, being persecuted isn't always fun, but it sure beats spending eternity in hell. Sometimes people make fun of or even hurt us for living for Christ, but He saved us, died for us, and we will never regret choosing to follow Him. Look at the end of verse 11. People that do not like us will come and go, but Christ is with us forever! Let's not be swayed by a temporary challenge. Live a godly life! That brings eternal rewards!

***Who are you afraid of? Do you want to please man more than you want to please God? Are you looking for God to rescue you from trouble?***

Tuesday 2 Timothy 3:13-17

Q:

A:

Digging Deeper

Don't you hate it when the fun stops? When a great movie comes to an end, don't you wish it would keep going? Unfortunately, many of us approach our walk with Christ like that – we just stop. We do well for a while, but we stop. That's terrible! Verse 14 was the key for Timothy. *Keep on! Continue! Trust God* to give you the strength to keep going! We find that strength in His Word. How often is our time with God the first thing to go when we get busy or weary of living for Him? When we do that, we unplug ourselves from the power source, and everything goes downhill from there! His Word equips and empowers us for right living (v. 17).

***If you're struggling in your Christian walk, are you focused on His Word? What are you depending on besides God's Word for strength?***

Week 51

Wednesday 2 Timothy 4:1-4

Q:

A:

Remember, this is the last chapter of the Bible that Paul ever wrote. Of all things he could choose to say to Timothy, Paul says this – *Preach the Word.* Check this out. The word *preach* here doesn't necessarily mean to preach a sermon from the pulpit. It just means *to proclaim*, or *to say out.* This isn't just for Timothy or pastors. It's for all of us. God's Word should penetrate all of our speech. We just can't help but talk about His Word. No matter where, no matter what – just lovingly share God's Word. Yes, there are people that don't want to listen, and that's their choice. We don't force them, but there are plenty of people that do want to hear. Who knows when the fruit will be ripe for harvesting?

***Does the Lord often come up in your conversations with people? Commit to sharing one thing from God's Word today with someone.***

Thursday 2 Timothy 4:5-8

Q:

A:

A *drink offering* is a type of sacrifice from the Old Testament. It was something that was set aside for God, and then completely poured out. That's how Paul saw himself. He knew he was going to die, and his life was one that was *poured out* to God for His glory. He didn't waste his time on earth. He did what God wanted him to do. If there is one thing we want to be said of us it is, "We finished well." Paul compares life to a race. We don't know how long our race is, but what would be said if your *race* was over tomorrow? Would people look on and say, "He gave Christ his all. He finished well."

***Name one area in your life that you could improve. What are you going to do to grow in that area? Would you ask another Christian to help you?***

Life stEP

Friday 2 Timothy 4:9-15



Q:

A:

Digging DEEPER

Paul wanted to see Timothy one last time. He told him to come quickly because Paul's execution was not far off. Unfortunately, we learn about Demas here. Demas was a Christian who left Paul to follow his own wants. Wouldn't it be terrible to be known throughout the rest of history as the guy who deserted the great Apostle Paul! Unbelievably, there's another one in this passage who also deserted Paul – Mark. It happened in Acts 15. However, we do know that Mark later on must have had a change of heart and pursued Christ. He had really changed. So much so, that Paul wanted to see him again before he died. We all make mistakes, but once again the question is – "How did we finish?"

Life stEP

*Have you made a mistake you have not made right yet? Is there a relationship that you need to make right?*

Saturday 2 Timothy 4:16-22

Q:

A:

Digging DEEPER

What does it mean to be alone? Maybe you have a job that is boring and there's no one to talk to. Maybe you and your best friend only have one class together in school. What if you had tons of friends, but they never talked to you. One last time… Paul is in prison, waiting to be executed, everybody left him, and he's still not alone. For a Christian, being alone is impossible. It might feel like you are alone, but it's not true. This is what Paul said, "the *Lord* stood with me, and strengthened me." No, it's not the same as having a real person beside you. It's better! The Lord can protect, comfort, give peace, and love better than anyone else.

*Do you pray and spend time in His Word when you are lonely. Would you commit to doing that next time you feel alone?*

Week 52

Two Old Testament prophets - when was the last time you read these books and understood them? One thing is clear this week. You can't live part of your life for God, and part of it for yourself. There are always consequences! You'll study everything from animal guts to the destruction of entire cities. Check it out!

Prayer Focus for this week:

**Q: The QUESTION - What is the writer saying?**
**A: The APPLICATION- How can I apply this to my life?**

Sunday Nahum 1:1-15

Q:

A:

Digging Deeper

Nineveh? Sound familiar? Yep. The prophet Jonah went to the same city 100 years earlier than Nahum. God was merciful before, but not any more. Nineveh was the capital of the country that destroyed Israel. It was amazing that God spared them during Jonah's day! Even though it was such an ungodly city, God graciously spared them because they repented. They deserved destruction when Jonah came to them. Verse 9 says affliction (trouble) will not come a second time. It doesn't need to. This is the one, only, and last time. Nineveh will be destroyed. Verse 3 sums up today's passage well.

***How has God been gracious not to punish you as you deserve? Have you asked forgiveness? Are you changing?***

Life stEP

Monday Malachi 1:1-14

Q:

A:

Digging Deeper

Have you ever had a question for God? Did you ever wonder why life is confusing at times? People who listened to Malachi felt the same way. They didn't understand why God was doing what He was doing. This book covers 23 questions and answers. The people of God had questions for Him, and He responded. It turns out that life wasn't as difficult as those people thought. God's answers are straightforward. Most of today's questions were ones the priests would ask. We wonder, "Why didn't they just do what the Lord wanted?" Verse 14 is the key. They lived a very careless life toward God. They were casual Christians.

***Are you concerned what God thinks regarding everything you do? In what area of your life are you casual with God? What are you going to do to change that attitude?***

Life Step

Tuesday Malachi 2:1-9

Q:

A:

Digging Deeper

*Levi* refers to the very first group of priests. Malachi's priests were not obedient. They made animal sacrifices to God, and then took the guts outside the city and got rid of them. Disgusting? Even worse is what the Lord said He would do with these priests (v. 3). That's disgusting! God was going to eliminate them because they had no desire to honor Him. They were leading the people away from Him. That's why God would do something so gross. To dishonor God with your life is a big deal! Honor Him in all you do.

***What area of your life is not honoring to God? Do your actions point people to God or away from Him? Do your friends look to you to find answers about God?***

Life Step

Digging Deeper

One word describes today – *Duh!* Verse 13 mentions the Lord was not listening or accepting their offerings. "I thought the Lord always listens to prayers, and people that are sincere?" Two major sins Israel was committing caused the Lord *not* to listen (vv. 11 and 14). It's like a little boy standing in front of his mom with chocolate cookies all over his face. When asked what happened to the cookies she told him not to touch, he replies (with his mouth so full he can barely say the words), "I don't know." Israel wanted to enjoy their sin, but still expected God to bless them. That doesn't honor God. *Duh!*

***Will you remember to confess sin before asking God for His help? Are you trying to live with one foot in the world, and one foot in Christ?***

Life stEP

Thursday Malachi 3:1-6

You have to remember the last line of verse 17 before you jump into chapter 3. Where is God's justice? Chapter 3 is a prophecy that tells how Jesus Christ (the Judge) will come. The first time (Jesus in the Gospels) He came as the Savior. The second time (future) He'll come as the judge, and someone will prepare the way for Him. The question "Where is God's justice?" was a mockery. They thought they could sin and not be punished. They thought God didn't care. One day, our works will be judged, whether we are saved or unsaved (2 Corinthians 5:10). A Christian won't be judged as to whether he will be sent to hell, but will lose rewards for not living for God.

***What is the thing you think you got away with, but know God really saw? What are you going to do to make it right? Will you be ashamed at His coming?***

Life stEP

Friday Malachi 3:7-15

Q:

A:

Digging DEEPER Ever said something *in your heart* to God? You didn't pray the words verbally, but in your thoughts you did. The nation of Israel said things *in their heart* to God. "We do not rob God," and "It's useless to serve the Lord." Perhaps they didn't say these words out loud, but they didn't obey God in the things He told them. He wanted to bless them, but they wanted to keep hold of what they had. They refused to tithe and give love offerings. They wanted it all for themselves. Little did they know the Lord would have blessed them with so much more if they had just obeyed. With their actions, they lived as if it was pointless to serve the Lord. Actions speak louder than words – especially to God!

Life stEP *Do you give to the Lord regularly? Do you serve God because you love Him or because of what you think you can get out of it?*

Saturday Malachi 3:16-4:6

Q:

A:

Digging DEEPER Chapter 4 describes what Jesus' judgment will be like for those who don't know Him. In yesterday's quiet time, Malachi spoke for the Lord and said "Return to me, and I will return to you." Most of the people didn't take that advice, but in verses 16-18 we learn of a few who did. There are two groups of people in the book of Malachi: those who did evil and didn't care what God thought, and those who feared the Lord. Those two groups still exist today. Who are you following? Many of your friends will live for themselves and ignore God (like the people in Malachi did). Verse 4 will help us to be like the people in verses 16-18.

*What would the Lord say about your life so far? How often do you remember God's Word throughout the day?*

**The following chart is provided to enable everyone using Word of Life Quiet Times to stay on the same passages. This list also aligns with the daily radio broadcasts.**

| | | |
|---|---|---|
| week 1 | Aug 27 – Sep 2 | Psalms 1:1-7:8 |
| week 2 | Sep 3 – Sep 9 | Psalms 7:9-11:7 |
| week 3 | Sep 10 – Sep 16 | Psalms 12:1-17:15 |
| week 4 | Sep 17 – Sep 23 | Psalms 18:1-21:13 |
| week 5 | Sep 24 – Sep 30 | Psalms 22:1-25:22 |
| week 6 | Oct 1 – Oct 7 | Ephesians 1:1-2:22 |
| week 7 | Oct 8 – Oct 14 | Ephesians 3:1-4:32 |
| week 8 | Oct 15 – Oct 21 | Ephesians 5:1-6:24 |
| week 9 | Oct 22 – Oct 28 | Esther 1:1-5:14 |
| week 10 | Oct 29 – Nov 4 | Esther 6:1–S of S 6:3 |
| week 11 | Nov 5 – Nov 11 | Titus 1:1–Philemon 25 |
| week 12 | Nov 12 – Nov 18 | Revelation 1:1-2:29 |
| week 13 | Nov 19 – Nov 25 | Revelation 3:1-6:8 |
| week 14 | Nov 26 – Dec 2 | Revelation 6:9-10:11 |
| week 15 | Dec 3 – Dec 9 | Revelation 11:1-14:7 |
| week 16 | Dec 10 – Dec 16 | Revelation 14:8-17:18 |
| week 17 | Dec 17 – Dec 23 | Revelation 18:1-20:6 |
| week 18 | Dec 24 – Dec 30 | Revelation 20:7-22:21 |
| week 19 | Dec 31 – Jan 6 | 1 Kings 1:15-11:13 |
| week 20 | Jan 7 – Jan 13 | 1 Kings 11:41-18:16 |
| week 21 | Jan 14 – Jan 20 | 1 Kings 18:17-22:40 |
| week 22 | Jan 21 – Jan 27 | 2 Kings 1:1-5:16 |
| week 23 | Jan 28 – Feb 3 | 2 Kings 5:17-9:37 |
| week 24 | Feb 4 – Feb 10 | 2 Kings 13:14-23:3 |
| week 25 | Feb 11 – Feb 17 | John 1:1-3:12 |
| week 26 | Feb 18 – Feb 24 | John 3:13-5:14 |
| week 27 | Feb 25 – Mar 3 | John 5:15-6:58 |

| | | |
|---|---|---|
| week 28 | Mar 4 – Mar 10 | John 6:59-8:24 |
| week 29 | Mar 11 – Mar 17 | John 8:25-10:13 |
| week 30 | Mar 18 – Mar 24 | John 10:14-12:11 |
| week 31 | Mar 25 – Mar 31 | John 12:12-14:14 |
| week 32 | Apr 1 – Apr 7 | John 14:15-16:33 |
| week 33 | Apr 8 – Apr 14 | John 17:1-19:22 |
| week 34 | Apr 15 – Apr 21 | John 19:23-21:25 |
| week 35 | Apr 22 – Apr 28 | Proverbs 1:1-3:18 |
| week 36 | Apr 29 – May 5 | Proverbs 3:19-5:23 |
| week 37 | May 6 – May 12 | Hebrews 1:1-3:19 |
| week 38 | May 13 – May 19 | Hebrews 4:1-6:20 |
| week 39 | May 20 – May 26 | Hebrews 7:1-9:10 |
| week 40 | May 27 – Jun 2 | Hebrews 9:11-10:31 |
| week 41 | Jun 3 – Jun 9 | Hebrews 10:32-11:40 |
| week 42 | Jun 10 – Jun 16 | Hebrews 12:1-13:25 |
| week 43 | Jun 17 – Jun 23 | Lamentations 1:1-5:22 |
| week 44 | Jun 24 – Jun 30 | 1 Corinthians 1:1-3:15 |
| week 45 | Jul 1 – Jul 7 | 1 Corinthians 3:16-7:9 |
| week 46 | Jul 8 – Jul 14 | 1 Corinthians 7:10-10:11 |
| week 47 | Jul 15 – Jul 21 | 1 Corinthians 10:12-12:20 |
| week 48 | Jul 22 – Jul 28 | 1 Corinthians 12:21-15:11 |
| week 49 | Jul 29 – Aug 4 | 1 Corinthians 15:12-16:24 |
| week 50 | Aug 5 – Aug 11 | 2 Timothy 1:1-2:26 |
| week 51 | Aug 12 – Aug 18 | 2 Timothy 3:1-4:22 |
| week 52 | Aug 19 – Aug 25 | Nahum 1:1–Malachi 4:6 |